D0840983

ME, TOO!

Child and Adult
Sexual Abuse
And
Prevention

Susan Sophie Bierker, MSW

Printed in the United States of America

ISBN: 978-1-939237-58-3

Published by Suncoast Digital Press, Inc.

Sarasota, Florida, USA

CONTENTS

DEDICATION

To Ellen
My Dear Sister, With Love

FOREWORD

John F. Salveson

I have never written a book Foreword before, but I'm pretty sure I know why I was asked to write this one.

I am a survivor of clergy sex abuse and a former patient of Susan Bierker. I have been working to expose child sex abuse, its perpetrators and enablers, since 1980. I have been very public about my abuse, my recovery, and my frustration with trying to hold people and institutions accountable for their decades-long sexual abuse of children.

I led the Philadelphia Chapter of SNAP (Survivors Network of Those Abused by Priests) for a while and served on the SNAP National Board. In 2005 I founded the Foundation to Abolish Child Sex Abuse to push changes in the legal and criminal justice systems to protect children from sex abuse. I do what I can to support anything and anyone who shines a light on this horrific problem, and Susan Bierker has certainly done that. So I will share a bit of my story, and tell you why I think this book is so important.

The first time I was sexually abused by Father Huneke I was 13 years old, traveling with him out of town. He came into my bed at night and began to perform oral sex on me. I froze and had no idea what to do. I was terrified.

The next morning, over breakfast, he told me what "we" shared was God's plan for us and was holy and an expression of his love. That morning, and for the next seven years as the abuse continued, I felt somehow responsible for what was happening. I hated it, it made me sick, I had no idea how to stop it – but I felt complicit. It literally never occurred to me in those seven years to tell anyone what was happening – a parent or friend, the police – no one. I felt trapped, completely alone and hopeless.

I made it through those years with lots of alcohol and by creating what I've come to think of as my second self – the person I presented to the world.

I did well in school, was an editor for the newspaper, played sports and graduated near the top of my class. Any parent would have been proud to have me date their daughter. But the real person inside was constantly anxious, trying to avoid the priest who controlled me. I began to drink as much as I could and became depressed and suicidal. In retrospect I think I was behaving pretty much as any person would in my situation.

I have often wondered, as an adult, why no one in my life suspected I was being sexually abused. I believe the answer to that question is a bit complex, but I am certain that a big part of it is that people had no idea how to identify suspected abuse and what to do about it.

I don't know what I would have done if someone asked me directly if I was being abused. But I am sure it would have necessarily changed the trajectory of my abuse – no matter how I responded. It would have given me a chance to disclose what was happening, or maybe just to consider the possibility that someone could help me.

Child sex abuse is hard to speak about, hard to think about and just plain horrifying. None of us want to believe that parents, priests, family friends, siblings – whomever – are capable of destroying children's lives in this way. But speak about it we must. Every chance we get. Because if there is one thing I have learned over these 35 plus years as an advocate and agent of change it is this: Sunlight is the best disinfectant.

So I encourage you – or maybe implore you – to read this book and learn about sexual abuse and how to stop it. I have always believed that there is probably no way to prevent an initial instance of abuse. But it is possible to prevent the second instance of abuse. If you know what to look for and open your mind to the possibility that something unspeakable may be happening to a child you know, you have a shot at stopping the second incidence of abuse. It takes courage to act, but it also takes knowledge. This book will give you the knowledge. The courage you will have to find yourself.

PREFACE

According to the National Sexual Violence Resource Center, April has been Sexual Assault Awareness Month since 2001 in the United States. The move to issue a proclamation observing the month was first started by President Barack Obama in 2010, and the tradition has carried over into the Trump administration.

"Sexual assault crimes remain tragically common in our society, and offenders too often evade accountability. These heinous crimes are committed indiscriminately: in intimate relationships, in public spaces, and in the workplace," the presidential proclamation from the White House stated in late March of 2018 to bring attention to Sexual Assault Awareness Month.

Over the past year, there has been a reckoning in the United States over sexual assault and harassment, particularly in the workplace, known as the #MeToo movement.

"#MeToo" is an internet campaign that circulates on Twitter and other social media platforms. Actress Alyssa Milano, and then millions of other people, urged survivors of sexual assault and sexual harassment to post "Me, Too" to raise awareness and highlight its pervasiveness. The encouragement for everyone to post publicly helped to de-stigmatize being a victim.

You may not know that "me, too" first appeared over ten years ago in the context of "not feeling alone" as a victim of sexual assault. A courageous and committed woman, Tarana Burke, herself a survivor, spoke as an activist to "end rape culture" wearing a t-shirt boldly imprinted with "me too," a phrase she had been using to bond with other survivors.

Milano acknowledges Burke as the originator of the meme which she has taken to an astronomical level of exposure. Her tweet on October 15, 2017, said, "If all women who have been sexually harassed or assaulted wrote "Me, Too" as a status, we might give people a sense of the magnitude of the problem." People (women and some men) came forward and posted who had experienced sexual harassment as adults, while many also noted the sexual abuse that they had experienced as children. Within hours of posting, the hashtag was the top trending topic on Twitter, where many other users, including celebrities and other public figures, were tweeting their own #MeToo stories. The post also quickly made its way over to Facebook where over 7,000 users had posted under the #MeToo topic within 12 hours. Coverage of the hashtag was subsequently done by online news organizations such as *CNN* and the *Huffington Post*.

The publications noted the connection between the topic and the then-breaking news of the Harvey Weinstein scandal. Weinstein, a famous film producer, was accused of sexual harassment and assault by multiple women. On October 15, 2017, Twitter published a Moments Page on the hashtag, which received more than 4,000 likes in 24 hours. The tweet posted in the wake of the Harvey Weinstein sexual assault allegations included sexual assault testimonies from other Hollywood actresses earlier in the month. Within one day the post received more than 38,000 comments, 13,000 re-tweets, and 27,000 likes. Since that time the #Me Too movement has gained strength and members.

It was then followed by "Times Up," started by well-known women in Hollywood who formed a group for women who had been sexually harassed and assaulted. The "Times Up" movement has expanded in support and membership.

Several events have happened since then to further the movement. In the December 18, 2017 issue, *Time* magazine awarded the "Persons of the Year" to "The Silence Breakers." On the front cover five women were pictured who are known as "The Silence Breakers" because they have come forward to talk about being victims of sexual harassment and sexual assault. Their bravery has encouraged countless other women to come forward. In January of 2018, the 75th Golden Globe Awards were dominated by powerful speeches by women who are well-known in the entertainment field, including Oprah Winfrey, about the prevalence of sexual abuse in their fields. "For too long," Winfrey said, "women have not been heard or believed if they dared to speak their truth to the power of those men, but their time is up."

Many of those present wore black clothing in solidarity with victims of sexual abuse. During the Grammy Awards that same month (also with a large television audience), dozens of artists and musicians sported white roses in support of the Me Too and Times Up movements. On March 8, 2018, at the Academy Awards, well-known actors and actresses gave speeches calling for clear and specific calls for change in the entertainment industries for everyone. All of these events have raised the consciousness of millions of men and women and have expanded the encouragement to women to use their power. More information on these above historic events is given in the second chapter of this book.

It is beyond extraordinary that Milano's call to action has had such a profound effect on the uncovering of the extent of sexual assault and harassment in our country (and some posts originate in other countries). At last, the taboo closet where we were keeping our past and present sexual abuse has been opened. Since Milano's post, there has been an overwhelming reaction by many celebrities and others who have come forward and told their stories. As a result of the "Weinstein Effect," there have been an incredible number of allegations and accusations reported. In Chapter 1, I list many of the accused and consequences of the allegations which include firings from jobs, retirement and criminal prosecution. By no means is this a full list—I hope you will find this and all the facts in this book educational and that you will better understand that you have the power to eventually reduce the number of people on lists like this in the future.

The list continues to grow and if you wish to follow up, I have included a number of resources you can investigate. The names are mostly of men, from all professions and industries. You will read about Dr. Larry Nassar, the doctor who sexually abused over 500 girls in his capacity as part of the medical staff for Olympic Gymnastics and Michigan State University and is now in prison for the rest of his life. In March of 2018, Wikipedia published a report, "2017-18 United States Political Scandals," which lists 41 political figures who have been accused of sexual misconduct, including sexual harassment and sexual assault, and subsequent firing and resignation of American politicians. The politicians are from the Executive Branch, United States Senate, United States House of Representatives, a Federal Judge and numerous State politicians. Needless to say, during 2018 there will be many special elections held to fill the seats of those who have been fired, who resigned, or who retired. It is distressing to know how many of the people we elect are sexually abusing others; however it is good that some have finally been identified.

I have been researching and writing on this particular topic for many years. With "me, too" bringing about so much awareness and concern, I felt compelled to complete my research and fulfill my commitment to help as many people as possible understand and be educated about sexual abuse. In my 20-year practice as a Clinical Social Worker psychotherapist, I specialized in treating and helping clients heal who were child victims and adult survivors of sexual abuse. They were devastated, disoriented, and dysfunctional as a result of their sexual abuse experiences and it was my joy to help them heal and go on to live fuller, happier lives. I have had a very fulfilling Life Coaching practice since coming to Florida helping sexual abuse victims became not only survivors, but thrivers as well. I feel my mission in life is to help those who are hurting and confused to heal and move on with their lives, and to do so joyfully.

Education is prevention. This book will teach you how to keep yourself, your children, and others as safe as possible from sexual predators—from being violated at the level of workplace harassment up to the extremes of incest and rape. Of course my heart and yours goes out most sympathetically to innocent children. Protection starts with awareness and education, the essence of this book. If we are able to tell our kids how to avoid being sexually abused, or we learn how to detect it if it has already happened, perhaps we will preserve their chance for safe, formative years—and lessen the number of people growing into adulthood carrying the deep scars of childhood abuse.

Whether you are interested as a concerned parent or community member, or as an adult carrying the scars of sexual abuse, my intention here is to give you knowledge, understanding, and hope. With confidence from my experience as a therapist, I can show you that there is a process to heal, a way to stop letting the past dictate your present life, and that you can move on as a survivor, no longer a victim.

In addition to professional examples, I also have a personal victory to share with you. Yes, me, too. Through years of therapy (group and individual) I am blessed that I am now a sexual abuse survivor. I have been very challenged to write this book, as doing so brings up my pain around my own sexual abuse as a child. I have been very fortunate throughout the years to have therapists who have helped me with the after effects of the sexual abuse, but it would be unrealistic if I thought that there are no vestiges of my issues. Healing is a lifetime journey no matter how much

I want it all to go away. I now have the tools to help myself, and know to go to my therapist if I am triggered, which helps considerably.

In the past, many of us have not told anyone about our sexual abuse because we felt ashamed and guilty that we somehow caused it or were party to it. Because we kept it secret, the perpetrators were able to continue victimizing us and/or others. It is interesting that some of the "me too" people are not only ridding themselves of toxic secrets but naming names. And remember, the messages we see are only the tip of the iceberg. For every person posting a "me too" experience, there are many more who are not on social media, or who are choosing not to post the admission.

Since October 15, 2017, the media has been filled with accusations by women about harassment, verbal coercion, and even rape by Harvey Weinstein, a famous film producer. As horrible as the accusations are, we now know his behavior is not uncommon. Many of us share experiences of sexual harassment and sexual assault and have remained silent because of our guilt, shame and decision that nothing could be done about it—and that no one would care if we did tell. Or we were afraid of losing our jobs and livelihood if we objected to sexual harassment or became the whistle-blower.

I could not agree more with the growing trend to get the transgressions and transgressors out in the open. We women and men who have experienced sexual assault and harassment now, more than ever, have the opportunity to speak out and express our rage. We need to claim our power and bring into the light what has been ignored and excused for so long. Through social media, we can join with others for support and to express our feelings. And then we may choose to heal through therapy or support groups.

One anonymous comment I read said, "It took a lot of strength for the brave women of Hollywood and the entertainment industry to put their foot down to a social issue that is systemic in human culture. It takes tremendous courage to stand up against this type of oppression and intimidation. We all need to change the way we think about who and what is a predator. It's not just the stereotyped white male in power. They come in all shapes and sizes and their reach spans across all social cultural and economic backgrounds."

A recent tweet said: "For the past few days I have been thinking about all the uncomfortable situations I and/or my teammates have experienced throughout the years with trainers, doctors, coaches, executives, and even teammates. From inappropriate comments, unwanted advances and grabs of the ass to coaches and GM's and even press officers speaking about players 'tits' and physical appearance, sexual harassment is rampant in the sports world. I always felt I 'handled it' and stood up for myself in those situations, but there were never any consequences for the perpetrators. That needs to change. Silence will not change the world." #Me Too

Another internet comment said, "We now have an opportunity to speak up if we are being sexually harassed and assaulted. We need to speak up and not condone this behavior. By speaking up, we also protect others. Sexual assault and harassment are not respectful. We must do everything in our power to speak up about it and take actions to end it. We must take definitive action to change the culture where sexual assault and harassment are tolerated and hidden. Individually, you can take action, boost your confidence, stop apologizing, stop bystander blindness, and give up being deferential. If we, as a society, no longer stay silent or allow the threat of consequences to silence us, we can end it." Democratic Rep. Jackie Speier testified before a House committee soon after three lawmakers resigned in the span of three days because of allegations of sexual harassment of their staff members. She reported she, too, had been sexually harassed and co-sponsored a ME TOO Congress Act. The lawmakers are:

Rep. John Conyers Jr. (D-Mich.) on Tuesday, December 5, 2017, and on Thursday, December 7, Sen. Al Franken (D-Minn.) and Rep. Trent Franks(R-Ariz.) — None were criminally convicted, but all stepped down over multiple allegations of sexual misconduct or harassment.

Since that time there has been a surge of women running for office caused not only by the me too movement, but also because women are being encouraged to use the power they did not know they had. It seems that many women are finding the courage to compete with powerful, politically-experienced men and are fueled by a number of factors, resolute and righteous anger among them.

Could it be that an insidious trend is reversing? Are there enough brave souls speaking up? Is the growing intolerance at a societal level vehement enough to have a significant and lasting impact? Who doesn't want sexual abuse to stop? We all do, and we all have a responsibility to learn how to help. By you reading this book, you are taking an important step for this cause.

The time has come to finally, collectively, take a stand. It is time to stop ignoring, supporting, or staying asleep to sexual abuse. And is it time for victims to be honest with themselves and, when ready, with others who can be safe, compassionate, and helpful. We all have an opportunity to heal from our past and present and go on to lives that are not hampered by our sexual assaults and sexual harassments. Furthermore, we have a responsibility to do so, as our healing is part of the world's healing.

Though it may seem that there is always more and deeper healing work to do, I want all of us "me, toos" to heal our pain and take our power back. Even though this book-writing journey has been one of hills and valleys, I am on a mission to educate all of you about sexual abuse, because education is the way we can prevent sexual abuse. It is all covered in this book.

To summarize: Educate yourself. Pay attention. Help others. This is how you, like I, can be a Sexual Abuse Prevention Advocate. Please let me know if what you learn is helpful to you. I am on a mission!

CHAPTER 1

INTRODUCTION

Sexual abuse is a perennial feature of human life, having occurred as far back as historical record exists. Many people think of it as a temporary aspect of modern life, like fear of nuclear holocaust, because taboos against discussing it have only been lessened within the last ten years. Unfortunately, sexual abuse of children is widespread even though prohibitions exist against performing or discussing this emotionally devastating practice. Adults are victims, too. For the protection of the innocent, the laws that forbid victimizing anyone sexually need to remain in force. However, the taboo that forbids discussion of the subject must be broken and discarded like a rusty, useless chain which imprisons its victims.

I have spent thousands of hours with sex abuse victims. Beginning the treatment of a sexually abused child (or an adult survivor of sexual abuse) can be the most challenging and gripping moment of a lifetime. I may reach out to touch the victim and he or she may recoil just as if I had attempted to strike him. Even a gentle, verbal approach may elicit a parallel response of fear, pain, and mistrust. This behavior occurs because these victims have been deeply hurt emotionally; very often they have been physically harmed as well.

Engaging with victims is difficult, yet so rewarding because those of us who work with sexually abused persons know that they can be helped out of their painful world. We experience a great deal of empathy for the pain they have endured in the past, and the pain they experience as we treat them. If you or anyone you know has attempted to recover from abuse without the help of a professional, I have two pieces of advice: read this book, cover to cover, and talk with a mental health professional, even if you plan to only meet with them one time.

There is something about the soul-tearing experience of sexual abuse that warrants professional help, no matter how resilient, courageous, and strong the person. Of course having highly trained mental health professionals to help is not the optimum plan; my mission is to prevent such abuse, and this book is your invitation to join that effort.

The first task is to educate the general public about sexual abuse. The taboo that prohibits discussion can be broken by bringing the subject out of its dark hiding place into the light of day. This book will bring light to bear. It will provide help in overcoming the natural emotional blocks we all feel toward such trauma to enable a reader to cope with the subject, not only intellectually, but psychologically.

WHAT IS SEXUAL ABUSE?

Definition: All sexual touching between an adult and a child is sexual abuse. Sexual touching between children can also be sexual abuse if there is a significant age difference (often defined as 3 or more years) because of a power imbalance. Sexual abuse does not have to involve penetration, force, pain, or even touching. If an adult engages in any sexual behavior (looking, showing, or touching) with a child to meet the adult's interest or sexual needs, it is sexual abuse. This includes the manufacture, distribution, and viewing of child pornography.

Discussing this book with a friend, all of a sudden her face turned pale and her jaw tightened. She was having a flashback from childhood when an adult male friend of the family could not seem to take enough photographs of her and her younger sister. He said his hobby was photography, and he had a home dark room so he could develop his own photos. Her parents just accepted his camera-happy ways but my friend said she and her sister called him "creepy" and hated his constant intrusion into their every activity. Even though he didn't ask them to remove clothing, he got too personal, and they could sense it. She said it was no coincidence that she had shied away from being photographed her whole life, and absolutely hated being a photographed subject in a public social media post.

After she shared these memories with me we looked the man up on the internet. Documented sex offender. So while his actions with my friend would not be defined as sexual abuse, this is an example of how abusers can cause hurt that stays with someone forever, even if the behavior is just shy of the definition of abuse. Be aware!

Adult sexual abuse includes sexual harassment (unwanted touching or verbal derogatory sexual comments), acquaintance rape, marital rape, or other sexual touching or acts perpetrated by trusted perpetrators such as doctors, dentists, hospitals, clergy, teachers, relatives, and others.

The child lacks the emotional and physical maturity to resist what amounts to abuse of the older person's position of authority and power. Abuse, by definition, causes pain to the child at the time of the abuse and, unless the abuse is disclosed and dealt with, later in his or her life. The pain is related to the feelings of powerlessness, perceiving himself as "damaged goods" and blaming himself for the abuse. The older person who instigates the abuse is universally known as the "perpetrator" by experts in this field. The perpetrator uses his position of authority and power to coerce the child into engaging in the activity.

Sexual abuse of a child generally moves through increasingly intimate activity. Perpetrators carefully plan not only the abuse but also arrange for a private place in which to do it. Parents often give the perpetrator access to their child unwittingly. For example, they may allow their child to engage in group activities which are lead by an unknown perpetrator or will allow their child to become friends with an older person they do not know. (Of course, too many times the parents do know the abuser and they just presume trustworthiness, which is a mistake.)

Most often, child sexual abuse is a gradual process and not a single event. By learning the early warning signs and how to effectively step in and speak up, sexual abuse can be stopped before or shortly after the child is harmed. Adults must take the primary responsibility for prevention of child sexual abuse by addressing any concerning or questionable behavior which may pose a risk to a child's safety.

Unfortunately, some children do not have adults in their lives who are able and/or willing to protect them and he or she will be seriously harmed by sexual abuse unless another adult in his or her life is educated about sexual abuse and able to recognize the signs. That is why it is important for all of those who come in contact to be educated in sexual abuse. Education = prevention.

\#   \#   \#

HISTORY OF SEXUAL ABUSE

The Origins of the Sexual Abuse Taboo

There are many versions of the Bible which prohibit sexual interaction with a close relative. For instance, the Bible verse Leviticus 18:6 has been interpreted as:

New International Version- "No one is to approach any close relative to have sexual relations. I am the LORD"

King James Bible- "None of you shall approach to any that is near of kin to him, to uncover their nakedness.: I am the LORD"

Even primitive tribes practiced the incest taboo, which was in force before recorded history. No one knows for sure why the most primitive societies believed sexual abuse of children was against natural law. Bad fortune, such as famine or other tribal or personal misfortunes, was believed to be the consequence of breaking the taboo. Also, tribal leaders did not approve of sexual relationships between members of the tribe because of the possible jealous feelings which would be created. Dissension of this nature might threaten to disrupt the group's solidarity and, therefore, its survival. The male tribal member was taught to seek intimate sexual partners in other tribes and bring these partners into his tribe for marriage.

How the Taboo Was Broken in Ancient Society

Just because the taboo existed many centuries ago does not mean that it was not broken. A taboo is merely an ideal. Drawings obtained from the Greek and Roman Empires depict nude children waiting on adults and also embracing them.

In ancient Greek and Biblical societies, sex between children and adults was tolerated and, in some instances, encouraged. Children were frequently used as prostitutes and were favored sexual companions in the Greek, Roman, and medieval societies. For instance, the Roman emperor, Tiberius, taught children to fellate him. In ancient Egyptian society, the incest taboos were broken to keep a family's bloodline "pure." For thousands of years there were intra-family marriages, especially those between brothers and sisters. There are countless historical examples of incest. Cleopatra is perhaps the best known pharaoh who married a sibling. Moses was born of a woman and her nephew. Abraham married his half-sister. Lots of daughters had intercourse with their fathers to perpetuate the human race. Ruling families in ancient Hawaii and the Incas of Peru practiced inbreeding. Eventually the practice was adopted by commoners in both Egypt and Persia.

History's Social Consequences of Breaking the Taboo of Sexual Abuse

Through the unfolding of the centuries, sexual abuse of children was taboo even as such abuse was actually practiced and, at times in some societies, even tolerated. However, the Greeks and Romans considered it to be inspired by the devil and the perpetrator doomed to hell, even as these societies tolerated the practice. One of the most poignant and greatest of the Greek dramas was *Oedipus Rex* by Sophocles. In this powerful play, Oedipus Rex and his mother, Jocasta, are separated when Oedipus is an infant. Oedipus is raised by someone his mother never knew. Fate leads him back to his mother because he longs for an older woman's (mother's) love. Jocasta is unconsciously searching for her lost son. Neither realizes they are related. They fall in love and marry. One day they discover their actual relationship. Tragically, Oedipus Rex tears his eyes out and Jocasta commits suicide. Obviously the creation and success of this great play shows that the ancient Greeks sought to discourage incest because of a social consciousness about its psychological consequences.

Various popes have been deposed through the centuries for incest. For instance, Pope John XII was deposed in 963 after being accused of incest with his mother and sisters. Pope Alexander VI was removed in 1492 because of sexual relationships with his daughter and son (he was also the father of one of his daughter's sons). Pope John VIII was also removed as pontiff for incestuous activities. The Catholic Church has prohibited sexual contact among the clergy up through modern times.

The Emergence of Public Recognition of Sexual Abuse

The Work of Sigmund Freud

The first time that the issue of sexual abuse was brought to the public's attention on a large scale was in the late 1800's when Sigmund Freud, the psychiatrist, developed his "Seduction Theory." After women patients came to trust him, many would reveal that they had been sexually abused by their fathers or other close relatives. Since Freud believed our actions were often based on our unconscious forces or wishes, he didn't believe these victims initially. He suspected they were merely expressing those wishes through fantasies because of their unconscious sexual desires for their fathers. He even named this concept an "Oedipus Complex," a term still used to describe the natural sexual and emotional attraction of a child to his or her parent of the opposite sex. The "Oedipus Complex" was named after the protagonist in the Greek drama, *Oedipus Rex*, described earlier. At about three years of age little boys fall in love with their mothers and little girls fall in love with their fathers. Since the parent of the same gender stands in the way, the child feels jealousy and wishes to eliminate his or her rival. At about five years of age the normal child realizes he cannot possess the sought-after parent.

Freud eventually believed his patients' testimonies that they had been sexually abused by male relatives. In private letters to friends, he identified fathers as sexual abusers and described how they seduced their daughters. However, he never felt comfortable writing publically about his discovery of incest. He felt that society would not be able to accept the fact that "respectable" family men were seducing their own daughters. He feared that such a disclosure would be harmful to his reputation since society would attempt to discredit him instead of accepting its own flaws. The clients' revelations proved that incest was quite common and even more threatening to society than was thought, since it was not confined to the mentally defective, poor, or illiterate.

Freud falsified incest case findings in a book he wrote in 1896 called "The Aetiology of Hysteria" in which he confirmed childhood sexual abuse and trauma, but identified the perpetrators as governesses, nurses, and seducers. Years later he admitted the seducers were not uncles, but actually fathers. He eventually repudiated the seduction theory altogether in 1897, reporting that sexual abuse of children did not exist at all. Freud feared society's reaction and subsequent disapproval, but part of the motive behind this repudiation was the discovery of his own incestuous feelings toward his daughter, which he revealed in letters to friends. He experienced these feelings suddenly, after her mother died.

Freud discredited his patients by saying their reports of sexual abuse were merely oedipal fantasies. In other words, their desire to have a sexual relationship with their fathers was so strong that they could not tell their fantasies from reality. In this way, daughters were brushed off as hysterical and were incriminated instead of their fathers. Unfortunately, Freud's repudiation allowed the entire subject of childhood sexual abuse to remain in the closet. Because society was too threatened by the concept to accept its existence and take aggressive action to stop it, children have continued to be victimized generation after generation. This "see no evil" mentality about sexual abuse exists even today.

Freud's repudiation reinforced the already-existing taboo and the fact that victims were thought to be delusional. As a result, many people hold the belief that children are fantasizing when they report that they have been sexually abused. This attitude has been ingrained into our culture although, fortunately, it is gradually changing.

The Treatise on Evidence

In 1943, a discussion of the subject of sexual abuse again appeared in the written form in the most famous legal text relating to abuse ever published in the United States. "The Treatise on Evidence" by John Henry Wigmore did further disservice to sexual abuse victims by again denying existence of abuse. In this widely read and respected text, Wigmore advised that the credibility of any female, especially a child, be disregarded if she complained of a sexual offense. Wigmore went on to write that women and girls are "predisposed" to making accusations against "men of good character." He, in essence, said that women who make sexual abuse allegations are delusional and that they need psychiatric treatment.

Wigmore's writing only reinforced Freud's, leaving abuse victims in limbo, again, and perpetrators safely behind their secret doors.

Alfred Kinsey's "Sexual Behavior in the Human Female"

In doing research on women's sexual behavior in the 1950's, including taboo subjects such as masturbation, extra-marital sex, and homosexual contacts, Kinsey stumbled upon another taboo subject unintentionally. He discovered the surprising fact that one-fifth to one-third of all adult females had experienced at least one sexual encounter with an adult male as a child, as the result of 4,000 personal interviews. Our culture still was not ready to absorb the full impact of these findings—a block that Kinsey's work reflected when he wrote that victims should not be upset by abuse experiences. He did not try to deny the existence of sexual abuse, but did brush off the devastating effects of victimization, even though 80% of the women interviewed reported they were very frightened and upset by the experience. In his book, *Sexual Behavior in the Human Female*, he writes, "It is difficult to understand why a child, except for it cultural conditioning, should be disturbed at having its genitalia touched, or disturbed at seeing the genitalia of other persons, or disturbed at even more specific contacts"

To add to the damage, he wrote that abuse was not the fault of the aggressor. He was very sympathetic toward perpetrators, who he felt could not help themselves. He viewed the perpetrators as victimized males in need of protection from malicious females, whether they be women or children. Thus, he expressed no sympathy whatsoever for the child victims. The public was just not ready to recognize sexual abuse as an emotionally damaging experience.

Finally, in the 1970's, the Women's Liberation movement brought the subjects suppressed by the taboo into the public consciousness. Subjects such as rape, wife-beating, and sexual abuse of children could no longer be suppressed. Since that time, child sexual victimization has been not only recognized, but studied and discussed in great detail.

HOW WE KNOW SEXUAL ABUSE IS UNNATURAL

The most blatant proof that abuse is unnatural is the very clear fact that the vaginas and rectums of children are too small for safe penile penetration; thus severe physical damage is very common. While less blatant in its obviousness, the emotional pain related to the long-term effects of abuse is an obvious proof of unnaturalness to anyone who believes happiness to be a natural state of mind. Children who are drawn into sexual activity suffer extreme long-term effects which hamper their self-esteem and ability to have healthy, intimate relationships as adults. Those of us who work with victims know that these behavior patterns are associated with emotional pain (depression) and dysfunction or limited sexual pleasure.

Here are some ways of looking at abuse and seeing the unnatural patterns of behavior and self-image it creates:

- Children do not have the emotional maturity to choose whether or not to have sex with an adult (we know, because of the pain abuse produces, that they would inevitably say no, given the choice). This teaches them submissiveness and an inability to

8

control what happens to their own bodies, which leads clearly to painful behavior patterns later in life.

- There is no concern for the child's welfare or his existence as a self-reliant, independent person. We know that victims who are taught in therapy to take charge of their bodies then experience great improvements in their ability to experience sexual and romantic pleasure and relief from depression. It becomes clear, then, that the perpetrator is doing nothing more than using the child in an almost animalistic, uncaring manner that produces the potential for long-term ill-effects.

- It becomes clear that children are simply unprepared emotionally for sex and cannot handle it in any way. Whenever they are denied freedom from involvement with sex prior to the time they can handle it, they suffer lasting ill-effects. Children who are drawn into sexual activity suffer extreme long-term effects which hamper their self-esteem and their future ability to have healthy, intimate relationships as adults.

HOW THE CHARACTER OF ABUSE DETERMINES THE DEGREE OF EMOTIONAL DISTURBANCE IT CAUSES

The degree of emotional disturbance to the child is more dependent on the relationships between the perpetrator and the child than on the type of sexual abuse. For instance, a child will probably feel a greater sense of betrayal and a break in trust if a beloved uncle is the abuser rather than a stranger. He will react more strongly if the uncle exposes his penis than if a stranger caresses the child's buttocks.

Intrafamilial sexual abuse means sexual abuse that occurs within the family. In this form of abuse, a family member involves a child in sexual abuse activities. The "family member" may not be a blood relative, but could be someone who is considered "part of the family," such as a godparent, neighbor, or very close friend.

When children are abused by adults who are supposed to protect them from harm, their ability to trust and rely on adults may be shattered. Knowing the the abuser is liked, or even loved, by other family members makes it all the more difficult for children to tell others about the abuse. Children who have been abused by a family member are more likely to blame themselves for the abuse than those who are abused by someone outside of the family unit. This is particularly true of older children, who may be all too aware of the effect that disclosing the abuse will have on other family members. As a result, it can take victims of intrafamilial sexual abuse weeks, months, or longer to let anyone know they have been abused and longer to reveal the details.

After disclosing, children and adolescents who have been sexually abused by a family member are often tormented by self doubt, self blame, fear of the abuser, and distress over what their disclosure has done to the family. Sometimes, in a desperate attempt to make everything better in the family, they may change their story or even deny that the abuse occurred. Taking back the disclosure is common and does not mean that children were lying about the abuse. When the abuse is caused by a family member, children may feel pressure to recant because of how the disclosure is affecting the family or because of lack of family support.

WHY THE RECOGNITION OF SEXUAL ABUSE IS TABOO

Even though there has been a great deal of exposure of sexual abuse in recent years, the taboo against the subject continues to flourish among the general population. This happens because of the factors discussed under the next two headings, which are the consequences of the taboo.

People Wish to Deny the Existence of Sexual Abuse

People have been brought up to believe that abuse is a terrible event. The taboos reinforce our natural disgust for abuse. Because even thinking about it is unpleasant, people would rather deny that it exists. If we deny the reality, then we don't have to do anything about the problem or accept the fact that there are children undergoing pain and hurt on a daily basis. This encourages children not to tell about the abuse they experience. Because of the secretive nature of sexual abuse, the actual high incidence remains hidden.

People Fear Their Own Incestuous Thoughts

Although most of us find the idea shocking, we all have felt an incestuous desire of our parents at some time in our lives. As parents, we all have felt some degree or incestuous feeling toward our children. That does not mean we are monsters or perverted. In fact, it's normal to have these feelings. However, most of us do not act on these feelings because we realize it would be immoral and damaging to do so. If we can accept that we are not demented for having these feelings, we can be more open to recognizing abusive situations which may exist around us. Acceptance of our natural wishes leads to greater receptivity to open discussion about this emotional laden area. As Freud so perceptively pointed out, we all store wishes we find unacceptable in our unconsciousness. We feel repulsion about the subject of sexual abuse as a way of keeping repressed incestuous desires out of the consciousness. However, the wishes are still there and they slip out in the form of remarks and behavior patterns. This results in a world in which most of us are at once fascinated by the subject and repelled by it. As a result, there is discomfort and confusion. Sometimes these ill feelings are handled by joking about the subject, i.e. "vice is nice but incest is best," or "incest, it's relative" or "incest is a game the whole family can play." These fears have been dealt with extensively by the media. Bringing out the fears may be helping people to break the taboo which surrounds open discussion of the subject.

Because of our fascination with sexual abuse and especially incest, there have been a number of films based on incestuous themes. "Chinatown," with Faye Dunaway, Jack Nicholson, and John Huston, profoundly expresses the perverted psychology of the perpetrator of incest. Huston plays Noah Cross, a multimillionaire who has conspired to corner the Los Angeles water supply. Dunaway plays Evelyn Mullray, whose husband is the water commissioner and who has refused to cooperate with Cross. When Mullray is murdered, his widow hires Jake Gittis, a private detective played by Nicholson, to find the murderer. Gittis falls in love with Evelyn. He eventually tracks down the plot to eliminate Mullray—and the existence of a daughter/sister Evelyn has produced with her father. (Cross is the father of his granddaughter.) In the final scene, it becomes obvious that Evelyn has for years concealed the whereabouts of the inbred child to keep her out of her father's hands, and thus spare her some of the pain she (Evelyn) experienced as a child when she was sexually abused by him. Cross tries to physically take the child from Evelyn's car, whereupon she shoots her father and flees. She is killed when police shoot at her as she drives away. Cross, even though wounded, makes his way to the stopped car and attempts to comfort the child and takes her into his arms.

Huston conveys at once the old man's sympathy for the horrified child and his profound sexual desire for her. One is left with the idea that he will probably sexually abuse his granddaughter as he did his daughter.

In the *Savage is Loose*, George C. Scott portrays a man whose son tries to murder him when the family is stranded on a desert island, so that the son can possess his mother sexually. The movie and the T.V. series, *Peyton Place*, by Grace Metalious, depicted a sexual relationship between a step-father and a step-daughter. Vladimir Nabokov writes of an older man pursuing a young girl sexually in the popular novel *Lolita*. Incestuous wishes were portrayed in films based on books and plays, such as *Sons and Lovers* by D.H. Lawrence, *Mourning Becomes Electra* by Eugene O'Neil, and *Cat on a Hot Tin Roof* by Tennessee Williams. In the movie *Sleep Walker*, based on a story by Stephen King, an incestuous mother and her son, portrayed as an evil super hero, are mutant cat people who need virgin blood to live. This homicidally–minded incestuous couple are portrayed tragically as they literally only have each other. Another Stephen King movie, *Dolores Claiborne*, gradually reveals the source of a mystery surrounding an adult daughter who has blocked out her memories of childhood sexual abuse by her father.

Love songs sung seductively by women to "Daddy" with verses such as "Daddy, You've Got to Do the Best for Me" or songs sung by a man about "Baby" may have incestuous roots.

The popularity of sexual abuse and incest as "entertainment" is puzzling, when you think about it. Like so many other taboos that the film industry pierced, these topics make people feel like they are watching "realism"— things that everyone knows exist but won't talk about; the viewer can identify with either the victim or the abuser in many cases, and doesn't feel as alone with their thoughts, emotions, and experiences.

HOW COMMON IS SEXUAL ABUSE?

According to the Center for Victims of Crimes website, one in five girls and one out of 10 boys will have been sexually abused before the age of 18. Many of those who treat abused persons, including myself, feel sexual abuse is even more common, since most incidents remain a secret. These are only intuitive guesses as it is impossible to do a statistically valid study because of the taboo which still exists on the subject. One aspect of the taboo is that people do not want to admit they have been sexually abused because they feel shame as if it were their fault, or they try their best to shut away and forget the incident(s) and have no desire to recall something in order to open up to others.

Also preventing real accuracy in knowing the prevalence of abuse is that it is impossible to go into a school system and ask the students if they have ever been sexually abused. If the superintendent of our imaginary school system allowed researchers access to children to question them about this issue, he probably would be fired immediately as a result of parental shock and disapproval. Many parents do not want their children "traumatized" by this "unsavory" topic. In some cases, this reaction results from the presence of sexual abuse in the home.

We cannot derive statistics from the number of incidents reported to authorities as most cases remain unreported. We know this because of the cases that are accidentally discovered and voluntarily disclosed long after the abuse occurs. The only method which seems able to work is to survey groups of adults about their sexual experiences as children. There has been no nationwide study which might provide us with more reliable statistics by including the widest possible sampling of victims.

The web site for Darkness to Light has very good statistics and information on sexual abuse statistics.

Is Abuse Increasing or Decreasing?

Until the late 1970's, the subject of sexual abuse was taboo. It was rarely discussed and our society denied that it even existed. As the taboo against recognizing sexual abuse as a reality began crumbling and the mandatory reporting of abuse was legislated, there was a leap in the number of people reporting its occurrence to authorities. As they began to hear about incidents of sexual abuse, many assumed that it had just begun to be a common occurrence. It is difficult to ascertain if sexual victimization was more common; however, we do know from talking with adults that abuse was common back then. There are some factors which have tended to cause a decrease in sexual abuse in recent years and others which may have tended to increase it, so it is difficult to say if it is increasing or decreasing.

Incidences of child abuse, including sexual abuse, have a profound effect on the lives of many children across the United States. Therefore, all states have set in place variations of mandatory reporting laws in order to decrease and prevent these incidents from occurring. These laws help ensure that cases of child abuse are reported to the proper authorities.

Mandatory reporting laws differ for each state when it comes to child abuse which includes physical abuse, sexual abuse, and emotional abuse. In some states these laws require that people in certain professions report child abuse to a proper authority, such as a law enforcement agency or child protective services. In other states, the mandatory reporting laws require that any person who suspects child abuse report any such instance. Professional mandated reporters are people who have frequent contact with children because of their occupation, such as teachers, employees of day care centers, social workers, physicians, dentists, licensed therapists, clergy members, and others.

Situations in which mandatory reporters must report vary depending on the state. Generally, reports must be made when the reporter has reason to believe or suspects that a child has been abused and when the reporter sees a child being subjected to harm or knows of conditions that would reasonably result in harm to the child.

Reporters should not be concerned about their identity being disclosed to the alleged perpetrator in a majority of states. However, many states require the mandatory reporter to provide his or her name and contact information as a part of the initial report. This information may be published to government officials who will be conducting the investigation. To find more child abuse information specific to your state, see Findlaws Child Abuse Information by State. If you are aware of or have any suspicion of child abuse, contact your local law enforcement agency or call the Childhelp National Child Abuse Hotline (800)422-4453, https://www.childhelp.org/hotline/.

People who fail to report child abuse or neglect can face penalties and consequences in state with mandatory reporting laws. These laws typically apply only to certain individuals who are in a position to discover sexual abuse. This can include teachers, medical professionals or law enforcement, among others. In states with mandatory reporting laws, those subject to the reporting requirements must report cases of suspected child abuse through a hotline or law enforcement agency. Failure to do so in a timely manner is considered a misdemeanor in most states and can result in fines, jail time, or both.

A Reason for a Possible Increase in Abuse

There are many reasons for a possible increase in the incidence of sexual abuse. Unfortunately, married couples in our society are becoming divorced at an alarming rate. Because children generally remain with their mothers, they can be more vulnerable to sexual abuse because there are more unrelated males who have access to the children. For instance, a mother may have male friends who are in and out of the children's lives, or she may re-marry. Then a step-father will come to live in the house full time. A male friend or stepfather may consider the children fair game sexually since there is no blood relationship. Children in a single-parent home or step-parent home are 10 times as likely to be sexually abused, according to some experts.

CHARACTERISTICS OF SEXUAL ABUSERS

Approximately 90% of all perpetrators are men. Women do victimize children occasionally but are much less likely to do so because of cultural expectations and possible inherent factors. Women have been socialized to fulfill more non-sexual needs in a relationship and are therefore not as likely to sexualize a relationship as a man. For instance, men are still the sexual aggressors most of the time and seem more able to have "one-night stands." Women are more likely to feel "used" in one of these brief sexual encounters.

Men are more likely to separate a sexual relationship from an emotional relationship. They seem able to relate just sexually at times and do not seem to need the emotional involvement women need. For this reason, men are able to relate sexually to children more easily. They are able to obtain some degree of sexual gratification even though the grown-up emotional relationship typical of adults who treat each other as equals is not present.

Men who have been sexually abused themselves as children may feel powerless and then are able to feel powerful when sexually abusing a powerless child.

According to recent studies, step-fathers are about five times more likely to enter an incestuous relationship with a child in the family than a natural father. Since friends of a step-father do not feel as much hesitation about abusing a friend's step-daughter as they would his real daughter, the friends are also five times more likely to abuse a family child if they are connected with the step-father rather than the natural father.

Socio-Economic Class

Perpetrators come in three-piece suits, coveralls, uniforms, or in any other attire. They can be a teacher, a well-known politician, a prominent attorney, a bank president, or a factory worker, mechanic or janitor. Some people have a pre-conceived notion that perpetrators will be noticeable by how they behave or dress or by their physical appearance. Not so. They are hardly crazed, "dirty old men" who are easily identifiable. Because they often give the impression of looking and acting like "respectable" citizens, we are shocked to find out that "Mr. Respectable" likes little boys in more than a friendly way, or that "Mr. Pillar of the Community" has intercourse with his step-daughter on a regular basis.

VICTIMS: RISK AND RESCUE

Some children are more likely to become sexual abuse victims than others. Lonely children with unmet emotional needs are easy targets. The perpetrator can pretend to love them and be interested in them to obtain sexual cooperation and to seduce them. These vulnerable children will not usually tell anyone about the abuse because they are afraid of losing the perpetrator's "love."

Children whose mothers are divorced are at greater risk of getting abused because of the potential of men coming into the home. Male perpetrators often date women who have children as a way to have easy access to these children. Some men are sexually opportunistic. A child is more likely to respond to one of these men if there is a poor or non-existent relationship with their natural father. Either young boys or girls may turn to a male perpetrator to make up for the absence of a strong male influence. A step-father is considered more likely to sexually abuse a child in a family situation than is a natural father. This is because he may feel free to over-step the incest taboo boundaries since he is not related by blood.

Those children without a close relationship with their mothers stand a greater chance of being in an incestuous relationship with their fathers than those who are close to their mothers. Because the mother is distant, the child (of either sex) attempts to meet unmet needs with the father and is more receptive to any advance he might make than he would otherwise be.

Further, a distant mother is not as able to protect her child from an abusive father for several reasons. Since there is poor communication between mother and child, the child is not as likely to tell her about paternal abuse; thus the distant mother may often be unaware of such activity in the home. Also, if the mother plays the role of a victim in the family, a daughter learns through role-modeling that females are expected to be submissive, powerless, and to obey. The message which is transmitted and learned by the girl is that females are not to object to being a victim, sexually or otherwise.

Mothers who are punitive and puritanical about sexual matters can raise daughters who rebel against their mother's blanket taboos. Such daughters are scolded for asking questions about their bodies or sex and the whole matter of sex is repressed in the household. The repression can backfire. In later life, such women may very well get themselves into sexually exploitive situations as a form of revenge against their mothers, and may be unconscious about the role their mother continues to play long after they live out on their own.

How Perpetrators Find Children and Adults to Sexually Abuse

Some perpetrators use the internet to find their victims. It's the world we live in today. Finding a bargain on a television you want is easier, and finding just the right person to target for sexual abuse is easier than ever before. The world-wide web is used by perpetrators for at least three distinct purposes. One may wish to lure a child for his own individual use to sexually abuse while others are recruiting children to be a part of sex rings, or to become part of a human trafficking organization. Luring children to be sexually abused on the internet grows more every year. Human trafficking is one of the fastest growing criminal industries in the world, both against children and adults. It is estimated that one out of seven children on the internet are solicited by a perpetrator on line.

A lone perpetrator uses social media to lure lonely and vulnerable children for sexual abuse and exploitation. The targeted children often use the internet because they are lonely and wish to reach out to other children in the chat rooms. Often the perpetrator poses as another child as a way of making friends with the child and gaining the child's trust. Often they trick the child into sending nude pictures of themselves or the perpetrator sends pictures of himself. Or the perpetrator may arrange a meeting with the child in a home, for example, and the child finds himself in a position to be sexually abused or kidnapped. A specific kind of perpetrator that is becoming more common is one who targets girls who are between the ages of 12-15, especially girls who are vulnerable and lonely. Very often these girls talk about their unhappy life and their desire to run away from home. You may wonder why a 14-year-old girl would agree to a secret meeting alone at a park or coffee shop with a 45-year-old man; she didn't agree to meet such a stranger. She thought she was getting a free "extra iPad" from a 17-year-old boy she had seen a photo of and had learned so much about "him" that he seemed more a friend than a stranger. Once she is out, alone, and disconnected from others, she becomes a target to approach or even kidnap.

Parents, educators, and anyone who has children in their care need to educate youth about internet interactions. Young people need to know that dangerous people use the internet to lure unsuspecting girls and boys to one-on-one meetings, posing online as another child or teenager. They need to know that the internet is a way for predators to find sexual prey.

Would you leave a child alone in a room full of sexual predators? And the door is closed? Of course not! The child's computer needs to be outside of the child's bedroom in a public area of the home. They need to be told to stop communication with any person who is getting personal and/or sexual. And that they are <u>never</u> to meet anyone off-line.

Pedophile Groups

There are groups of predators who often get connected on line but then meet together to sexually abuse one or several children. These groups are generally composed of men, sometimes professional men, who gather up children for sexual exploitation. Sometimes these men are married, have families, and are respected members of the community.

In Bucks County, Pennsylvania, five men were arrested in 2016 for sexually abusing a boy from 2009-2016, for multiple child rape, possession of child porn, and statuary sexual assault. During one rape, one of the perpetrators was dressed up in a red fox costume. Unfortunately, this is not an isolated case. I really do believe that we all have to educate ourselves and children about sexual abuse. We need to learn to recognize a child in distress and look further to find the reasons. Teachers and others need to learn what the signs of sexual abuse are and to teach children about how to avoid it. How many people came in contact with this boy in Pennsylvania over his years of being sexually abused?

Pedophile Advocacy Groups

The North American Man/Boy Love Association (NAMBLA) is a pedophile advocacy organization in the U.S. It works to abolish age-of-consent laws criminalizing adult sexual involvement with minors and campaigns for the release of men who have been jailed for sexual contact with minors that did not involve coercion. Members of NAMBLA say it is okay to sexually abuse male children, without even considering the damage to the child.

There are many websites where predators congregate. Two websites, Boy Chat and Annabelligh, are pedophile websites dedicated to adults who want to have sex with very young boys and girls. It is populated with pedophiles from around the world who discuss ways to groom little children for sex, and how to avoid getting caught by police and parents. They claim children love to have sex with adult men. Such sites are very disturbing and only emphasize how many very disturbed people there are who advocate sex with children.

Fortunately, there are many organizations who are working to reduce internet sexual crime. I am listing three of the very many. If you wish to go onto the internet, you will find many groups who are helping the victims of sexual abuse crime.

The Internet Watch Organization (IWF)

This organization works to make the internet safer by removing images of sexual abuse off the internet by very advanced technical means. They are an independent not-for-profit organization and work with global internet. They have 130 members, among them Facebook, Google and Microsoft, and work with them in keeping internet sexual abuse crime off of the internet. They have very sophisticated ways of monitoring sites for members.

Interpol

The International Criminal Police Organization, more commonly known as Interpol, is an international organization that facilitates international police cooperation. Internet sex crimes represent a huge challenge for the police worldwide and require specialized and increased resources. At Interpol they encourage investigators around the world to make maximum use of their tools and services. Their services are:

Victim identification—they work to identify the victims of sexual abuse depicted in photographs and films. Crucial to this work is the International Child Sexual Exploitation site in which their image database uses sophisticated image comparison software to make connections between victims and perpetrators.

Yellow Notices—at the request of a member country, Interpol can issue what they call yellow notice to help locate the missing person, especially minors. These notices are circulated on an international basis and recorded in Interpol's specialist group on Crimes Against Children. Formed in 1992, the group works with investigators around the world.

ICAC

Another group is the Internet Crimes Against Children Task Force Program (ICAC), which helps state and local law enforcement agencies develop an effective response to technology-facilitated child sexual exploitation and internet crime against children. They help encompass forensic and investigative components, training and technical assistance, victim services and community education. Since the ICAC program's inception in 1998, more than 589,000 law enforcement officers, prosecutors and other professionals have been trained on techniques and how to prosecute ICAC cases leading to the arrest of 73,000 individuals for internet crimes. This organization is under the US Department of Justice.

In 2014, the United States hosted the Global Alliance Against Child Sexual Abuse Online Conference. During that conference, 54 countries worldwide reaffirmed their commitment to fight online sexual abuse crimes. They shared technology and policies and issued this statement: "The threat to young people posed by online sex predators is on the rise. Challenges are constantly evolving. Every time a picture of an abused child is shown is how that child is being abused over and over again. The Global Alliance shows our collective willingness to fight this hideous crime, something we can only do by working together. Our collective promise must become a reality." The alliance shares electronic information and evidence held by internet service providers, with a commitment to: Facilitate prompt and comprehensive exchange among law enforcement of evidence and information; Enable existing, collaborative and transborder efforts to identify and rescue victims of online sex abuse.

It is reassuring that there are so many groups who are working so hard to reduce internet sexual crimes to protect innocent victims.

CHILD AND ADULT SEX TRAFFICKING

Under U.S. Federal law, sex trafficking is the coercion or forcing of a child or adult to participate in commercial sex against their will. Victims are sold to provide sexual services. This crime continues to grow at an alarming rate both in America and throughout the world. It is estimated that at least 20 million adults and children are enslaved and bought and sold worldwide into commercial sexual servitude. A definition of a child and trafficking organization is one who uses children and adults for prostitution, child pornography, child sex tourism and other forms of sex to have basic needs of shelter, food, and education met. They are isolated, intimated, and subject to physical and sexual assault by their traffickers. Most live under constant mental and physical threat. Many suffer severe emotional trauma, including symptoms of post-traumatic stress disorder and disassociation. They are at great risk of contracting sexually transmissible infections, included HIV/AIDS. Many become pregnant and are forced to undergo abortions.

Children used for commercial purposes are either kidnapped from any place or coerced or forced into joining trafficking organizations. Children are often run-aways or homeless youth who are found wandering the streets or hanging out at bus stations, truck stops or other public places. They are most often from homes where they have suffered from sexual, physical and/or emotional abuse. Members of the organizations aggressively recruit children, promising them food, shelter, drugs and money. They also promise gifts, a sense of belonging, and a place where they will be "loved"—at the same time grooming them for a life of prostitution.

Once they become a part of the organization, they are forced into prostitution and shoplifting. They are beaten and punished and are bombarded with violent threats, lies, and other forms of coercion to get them to participate in commercial sex. One of my friends in Pennsylvania was attending a workshop for Parents Without Partners many years ago and was staying at a hotel with her children. After people missed her, the police were called and they found her body in the trunk of her car. The children (ages 7 and 8) were never found...I wonder if they were kidnapped into one of these organizations.

Have you noticed that a child at a bus stop is often accompanied by their parent while they wait nowadays? That was unheard of when I was a child. More awareness and protectiveness like that is undoubtedly saving many of our children from abduction. It can happen to anyone at any time, and I have my own harrowing experience as proof. Years ago, my child's dad was walking with him in Manhattan. My small son was a few feet in front of his dad when a van pulled alongside and two men jumped out and ran toward my son. His father reached him and scooped him up just in time to save him. Even to this day, I become so frightened to think of how close one of my own children came to being abducted and possibly enslaved by a sex trafficking organization.

Adult women make up the largest group of sex trafficking victims, followed by female children, although there is a small percentage of adult females who are into the sex industry as well. Women who are victims of sexual trafficking are often those who are living in poverty and are not able to provide for themselves basic needs of shelter and food. Many have mental health issues and are unable to function on their own. They may not be able to hold down a job and do not have a good education. They most likely have a background of abuse, mostly domestic and childhood abuse. Some have a drug habit that makes them dependent on traffickers. So, while some people are kidnapped and enslaved, many more "voluntarily" participate out of desperation and fear.

Trafficking has a harrowing effect on the mental, emotional, and physical well-being of those ensnared in its web. Beyond the physical abuse, they suffer extreme emotional stress, including grief, distrust, and suicidal thoughts. Drugs and alcohol are often sought (and sometimes provided by the abusers) to numb the pain, and food and sleep are irregular and lacking. A person abducted into sexual enslavement loses their life. Too few are lucky enough to ever get it back.

Some sex trafficking is highly visible, such as street prostitution. But many groups are operating out of unmarked brothels in unsuspecting (sometimes suburban) neighborhoods. They may also operate out of a variety of public and private locations, such as massage parlors, spas, and strip clubs.

Fortunately, some of those involved as victims of sexual trafficking walk into freedom or escape and require dedicated assistance and love to restart their lives. Here in Sarasota, Florida, and throughout the United States, there are branches of the Selah Freedom non-profit organization dedicated to helping victims of sex trafficking.. This caring organization offers outreach as well as residential programs from which their grateful clients graduate to go on to independent and much happier lives. Their safe residential houses are located in Chicago and Wisconsin. Selah Freedom has the cooperation of local police, attorneys, and judges who help identify and support these victims as well as the legislators who work to establish better tools to fight human trafficking. Selah also offers a program for teens 12-17 within the school systems to educate the teens about sex trafficking so they do not get involved in it. Recently, a ticket agent at the airport got suspicious about two teenage girls who had first class one-way tickets to New York. They were going there because a man they met online wanted them to come there to audition for modeling jobs. Fortunately, the ticket agent blocked the girls getting on the plane. She then called the girls' parents who came and took them home. If the girls had gone to the hotel to meet the man they may have been kidnapped into sex trafficking. Education about sex trafficking is so very important!

President Trump signed new anti-sex-trafficking legislation into law in April, 2018. The new law, which passed congress with near unanimous bipartisan support, gives prosecutors stronger tools to go after sites such as Backpage.com. This site facilitated prostitution and revealed details about victims including minors as young as 14. Several of its top officials have been indicted. The new law will also let state law enforcement officials to pursue sites that knowingly host sex trafficking content, and will allow victims to sue such sites for damages.

CHAPTER 2

ALLEGATIONS AND CONVICTIONS

SOME MEN AND WOMEN ACCUSED
OF SEXUAL MISCONDUCT

THE WEINSTEIN CASCADE EFFECT

In early October, 2017, Harvey Weinstein, a high-profile Hollywood producer, was fired from his own company after multiple women came forward to accuse him of rape and sexual assault. The sudden cascade of sexual assault and sexual harassment allegations across the country began after the exposé of Harvey Weinstein and other men by the New York Times in October, 2017, in an article, "After Weinstein: 51 Men Accused of Sexual Misconduct and Their Fall From Power," along with the social media #MeToo movement. In the article, the men are listed in order of dates reported in the fields of finance, media, politics, entertainment, technology, and music.

The onslaught of reports is partly due to "The Weinstein Effect," similar to a domino effect, where one report inspired the next, and the next. Heavy media coverage encouraged those who had been silent until that time to now come forward. This was groundbreaking. Finally, the time had come for women and men who had experienced workplace sexual harassment to speak up, shattering the culture of silence that had always protected powerful men.

Public accusations of misconduct have revealed serial abusers who had been getting away with inappropriate, illegal, and harmful behavior, sometimes for decades. When Susan Fowler wrote her blog post in February, 2017, on the harassment she had experienced at Uber, the software engineer was somewhat of a lone voice in Silicon Valley But after accusations of sexual assault were leveled against movie mogul Harvey Weinstein in October, the #MeToo movement created a crescendo.

Ever since the New York Times initially published a staggering amount of on-record accusations against the embattled super producer, Harry Weinstein, dozens of women have come forward nearly every day to share their stories of similar treatment by powerful men in nearly every industry. Something appears to have changed. More and more women feel emboldened by the courage of Weinstein's accusers to tell stories they once may have thought would fall on deaf ears. After all, Weinstein's behavior was an open secret in Hollywood for decades, an intimidating yardstick for what men could conceivable get away with, until the day it suddenly wasn't. It's about time.

Sexual assault is motivated by hostility, power, and control. Sexual assaults are not motivated by sexual desire. Many of those accused have accumulated power and feel they can use it to control and overpower others. Also, sexual domination is used to increase a sense of being powerful among those who are actually feeling weak or comparatively less powerful than others they envy.

At the time of this writing, one or more accusations of sexual abuse comes out in the news nearly every day. Some of the reports are of recent incidents, while others go back many years. The #MeToo movement asserts it is never too late to speak up.

FOR ADDITIONAL INFORMATION:

1. Since the original report in the New York Times in October, 2017, listing the men who have been accused, The Times has published an updated report every month, adding even more high-profile men to the list.

2. The NBC news site published a report on January 10, 2018, titled "Since Weinstein, Here's a Growing List of Men Accused of Sexual Misconduct." This list contains a complete list of men who have been accused. The NBC list is mind-boggling with pages and pages of names, many recognizable due to their position in business or government.

3. The Times issued a report on November 9, 2017, and on January 26, 2018, titled "Here Are All The Public Figures Who Have Been Accused by Sexual Misconduct after Harvey Weinstein."

4. On February 4, 2018, NBC News posted an article, "Sexual Misconduct: A Growing List."

5. One of the most comprehensive articles is one on the CBS site, "The Dudes Accused of Sexual Misconduct and Sexual Harassment since Harry Weinstein …120 and still counting," which was published in February, 2018.

6. In Glamour Magazine, February 26, 2018, there is an article titled, "Post-Weinstein, These are the Powerful Men Facing Sexual Harassment Allegations," with a summary of those accused.

7. U.S. Weekly, March 1, 2018: "Hollywood Sexual Misconduct Scandals" has a summary of those accused.

If you wish to know more about those accused of sexual misconduct, you may refer to any of the above articles. For those who are accused in the future, even if the press tires of coverage, the internet is constantly being updated.

There's nothing new about powerful men being accused of sexual harassment. For years we have seen allegations against men at the highest levels of their respective fields—Bill Clinton, Father James Porter, Bill O'Reilly, R. Kelly, Louis CK, Woody Allen, Bill Cosby, Roman Polansky, and Donald Trump, just for starters. The unfamiliar part is that there are starting to be actual consequences.

These men are losing their jobs, being banned from future opportunities, and in some cases, are incarcerated, or legal action is forthcoming. Director Cameron Bossert had launched a Change.org petition to preclude Casey Affleck from presenting at this year's Academy Awards., due to allegations around his history with women; however, Affleck withdrew voluntarily. Perhaps best of all though is the consequence that men are hopefully taking a deep, introspective look in the mirror before ascending to positions of power in the future.

Perhaps the most hopeful sign of what has come from the outing of the men on this list is "Time's Up," the initiative started by famous women like Shonda Rhimes and Eva Longoria to help non-famous women get support when they have been sexually harassed. A lot of people have woken up to the fact that the sexual misconduct problems in Hollywood and the media are just the tip of the iceberg. Perhaps now the reckoning will trickle down.

As we wait to see the full extent of the fallout from the current tidal wave of charges, have a look below at a comprehensive list of powerful men accused of sexual harassment (and worse) in the wake of Harvey Weinstein.

This is a list of some of the most powerful men who have had allegations of sexual assault and sexual harassment. Some of the men lost their jobs, along with deals worth millions of dollars; others have had their reputations indelibly tarnished and may end up in jail. A few have taken their own lives. You may get additional details on these men by going to the websites listed above.

INDIVIDUALS WHO HAVE BEEN VICTIMS OF SEXUAL MISCONDUCT AND SEXUAL HARASSMENT

There are many women who have been sexually assaulted who have not reported the men since they were given large financial settlements without involving the legal process to keep quiet by signing Non-Disclosure Agreements. The NDA's generally have large penalties if the woman says anything to anyone about her abuse. There is no way to know how large this number is, but it is logical that there is a large number, especially since the high-profile men have the money and the strong aversion to having their reputation ruined. These victims sometimes receive settlements even before a complaint has been filed, while others receive settlements somewhere along the legal process. Congress has paid out more than 17 million dollars in settlements to federal workers under the Equal Employment Opportunity Commission from 1997-2017, according to a CNN report on November 26, 2017. The Politico website states in their article "How the Federal Government Hides Sexual Harassment Payouts" (1/3/18) that "Executive branch agencies have settled dozens of sexual harassment cases involving federal workers in recent years, but the resulting taxpayer funded payments are shrouded in mystery." As a result, what number of these settlements were for sexual harassment is uncertain. All of the settlements have been paid by tax payers.

There have been some very large settlements for sexual harassment that have gone through the court system.

- Ani Chopourian was paid 168 million dollars by Catholic Healthcare West in 2012—potentially the largest judgment in US history for a single victim of workplace sexual harassment.

- Ashley Alford was paid 6 million dollars by Arron's Rents (2011).

- Gretchen Carlson was paid 20 million dollars by Fox News for harassment by CEO Roger Ailes (2016).

- Anucha Browne was awarded 11.5 million dollars by Madison Square Garden (2007).

- Carla Ingraham was paid 10 million dollars by UBS Financial Services (2011).

- Lis Wiehl was awarded 32 million dollars for sexual harassment by Fox News host, Bill O'Reilly.

TRUTH AND CONSEQUENCES

Representative List of Men
Who Have Recently Been Accused (By Month)

September, 2017

Anthony Weiner, Former Democratic Congressman

Sexting underage girl, sentenced to 21 months in prison.

October, 2017

Harvey Weinstein, Producer and co-founder of Weinstein Company

Accusations of raping three women, sexual assault and harassment of dozens of others—including masturbating, exposing himself, and unwelcome touching. He was fired from his company and expelled from the Academy of Motion Pictures Arts and Sciences.

Andy Signore, Senior Vice President of Content for Defy Media

Accused of sexual assaualt of one woman and harassment of several others. He was fired.

Ray Price, Head of Amazon Studios

Accused of sexual harassment of one woman. He resigned.

Chris Savino, Creator Showrunner of "The Loud House"

Sexual harassment, including unwanted sexual advances, of as many as 12 women.

Cliff Hite, Ohio State Senator

Accused of repeatedly propositioning a female state employee. He resigned.

Robert Scoble, Tech blogger and cofounder of the Transformation Group.

Accused of sexally assaulting at least two women. He resigned

John Besh, Chief Executivew of the Besh Restaurant Group

Accused of sexual harassment. Stepped down.

Terry Richardson, Fashion Photographer.

Accused of harassment of models. Banned from working with Conde Nast.

Leon Wieseltier, a Former Editor at The New Republic

Sexual harassment of several women, including inappropriate advances. He was fired from Emerson Collective, which canceled publication of a magazine he was editing.

Knight Landesman, Publisher of Artforum

Accused of sexual harassment of at least nine women, including groping. He resigned.

Rick Nejera, Director CBS' Diversity Showcase.

Accused of sexual harassment, including inappropriate commens to performers. He resigned.

Mark Halperin, NBC News and MSNB contributor, co-author of *Game Change*.

Sexual harassment of at least five women. He resigned.

Raul Bocanegra, California State Assembly

Sexual harassment of at least six women. He resigned.

Kevin Spacey, Actor

Sexual assault of multiple men and sexual misconduct with a minor. He was fired from *House of Cards* and cut from other projects.

Hamilton Fish, President and publisher of The New Republic

Accused of complaints by female employees. He resigned

Michael Oreskes, Head of news at NPR and former New York Times Editor.

Sexual harassment of three women. He resigned.

Andy Dick, Actor

Sexual harassment, including groping. He was fired from film.

November, 2017

David Guillod, Co-Chief Executive of Primary Wave Entertainment Agency

Sexual assault of four women. He resigned.

Ray Moore, Alabama judge and Senate candidate (Republican)

Pursing relationship with and sexually assaulting underage girls. The Republican National Committee pulled out of a joint fundraising agreement. He lost the election for the Senate.

Benjamin Genocchio, Execute Director of the Armory Show Art Fair

Sexual harassment, including unwelcome touching of five women. He has been replaced.

Dan Schoen, Minnesota State Senator

Accused of sexual harassment, including sending a sexually explicit photograph. He resigned.

Louis C.K., comedian and producer

Sexual misconduct with five women, including exposing himself and masturbating in front of them. FX and other media companies cut ties. Movie release and comedy special were cancelled.

Andrew Kreisberg, Executive Producer of Arrow, Supergirl, The Flash

Sexual harassment of more than a dozen people, fostering a work environment in which women were demeaned and inappropriately touching colleagues including men. He was fired by Warner Brothers TV Group.

Eddie Berganza, Editor at DC Comics

Accused of sexual harassment of three women, including groping and forcibly kissing women. He was fired.

Tony Cornish, Minnesota State Representative

Sexual harrassment. He resigned.

Steve Jurvetson, Co-founder of a venture capital firm and a board member of Tesla and SpaceX

Accused of sexual misconduct. Resigned from firm and taking leave of absence from Boards.

Wes Goodman, Ohio State Representative

Accused of inappropriate behavior. He resigned

Al Franken, US Senator, Minnesota

Sexual harassment of several women, including forcibly kissing and groping. Resigned.

Glenn Thrush, reporter for New York Times covering the White House

Sexual misconduct. Suspended, and cannot cover White House anymore.

Russel Simmons, co-founder of Def Jam Records and other businesses

Sexual assault of two women. Later, four women accused him of violent sexual behavior, including raping three of them. Stepped down from his businesses.

John Conyers, Jr., US Representative, Michigan

Sexual harassment of several women who were employees. He retaliated against one employee who spurned his advances by firing her. He resigned.

Charlie Rose, television host

Sexual harassment of at least eight women, including groping and lewd phone calls. Fired by CBS and Bloomberg, and PBS canceled distribution of his TV interview show, *Charlie Rose.*

Johnny Iuzzini, chef and judge on ABC's *The Great American Baking Show*

Sexual harassment of four employees. Fired by CBS.

Matt Lauer, co-host of *Today*

Sexually inappropriate behavior with at least three women. Fired by NBC.

Garrison Keillor, creator and former host of *A Prairie Home Companion*

Inappropriate behavior with a co-worker. Dropped by Minnesota Public Radio.

Justin Huff, Broadway casting director

Sexual misconduct. Fired by his employer, Telsey Company.

Shervin Pishevar, venture capitalist

Inappropriate sexual behavior toward multiple women. He resigned from his top roles at Sherpa Capital and Hyperloop One. Two Democratic senators who received political donations from Pishevar said they would return the money by donating it to charities.

Israel Horovitz, playwright and founding artistic director of the Glorcester Stage Theatre

Accused abuse of nine women, some of whom were teenagers at the time. Theatre has cut ties and two plays were canceled.

December, 2017

Stephen Bittel, Florida Democratic Party Chairman

Sexually inappropriate comments and behavior. He resigned.

Ruben Kihuen, Member of the US House of Representatives, First Latino in House

Sexual harassment. Will not resign but will not run for re-election.

Peter Martins, Leader of New York City Ballet

Sexual harassment and physical and verbal abuse. He retired.

Matt Dababneh, California Assemblyman

Accused of sexual assault of several women. He Resigned

Danna Masterson, actor

Accused of raping four women. He has been fired from Netflix show, *The Ranch*. The Los Angeles Police Department is investigating the charges.

Lorin Stein, Editor of The Paris Review

Accused of inappropriate behavior, including unwanted touching. Romantically and sexually pursing women who worked at the Paris Review. He resigned.

Harold Ford, US Representative, Arizona

Harassment and intimidation of one woman. He resigned.

Trent Franks, US Representative, Arizona

Asked two female staff members to be surrogates to bear his child. He also made inappropriate advances towards women who worked in his office. He resigned.

Alex Kozinski, Federal Appeals Court Judge

Accused of sexual misconduct or inappropriate comments to female subordinates. Retired.

Ryan Lizza, writer for the *New Yorker* and political analyst for CNN

Improper sexual conduct. Fired from the *New Yorker*.

Mario Batali, chef, restaurant owner and co-host of ABC show, *The Chew*

Sexual misconduct, including inappropriate touching of four women, three who were employees. Was fired by ABC and stepped away from his businesses.

Donald Trump, President of the US

Accused of groping, fondling, forcible kissing sexual harassment. According to a story written by CNN, there was a press conference on 12/12 about three women who talked about their sexual experiences with Trump on the Megyn Kelly TODAY. These are part of a group of 15 women who have come forward accusing him of sexual misconduct dating back to 1970, all before he became president of the US. The first hand accounts came as a public conversation on sexual misconduct rages throughout the US. Nikki Haley, the US Ambassador to the United Nations, has encouraged these women to be heard. Two senators, Cory Booker of New Jersey and Jeff Merkly of Oregon, called for Trump to resign over the multiple accusations of sexual harassment and sexual assault against him. Many others are encouraging a Congressional Investigation. On the Wikipedia and Huffington Post (Article of 12/12/17) sites are a list of women who have accused Trump of sexual misconduct.

People magazine showed him in a picture with Natasha Stoynoff who claims he pushed her up against a wall and stuck his tongue down her throat. He denies he ever met her. The alleged incident took place in 2005 when Trump's wife was pregnant, according to the magazine.

In a report on February 7, 2018, Rachel Brooks, who has accused Trump of sexual harassment in 2005, has decided to run for office. Her allegations of sexual misconduct against Trump have been dismissed by the President, but she has a new approach to ensuring her message is heard—an attempt at a seat in the state legislature of her native Ohio. "I think my voice should have been heard then and I'll still fight for it to be heard now" she said. She says "Like many Americans, I have become disgusted with politics today…My situation with Trump… him not being willing to acknowledge his actions and his willingness to ignore what we had to say, that was sort of the last straw for me." President Trump denies all accounts by his accusers and no legally incriminating evidence has been produced to date.

Charles Dutoit, conductor

Sexual assault of four women. Withdrew from three scheduled concert series. Several major orchestras cut ties.

Marcelo Gomes, dancer at the American Ballet Theater

Sexual misconduct. He resigned

January, 2018

James Rosen, Fox News correspondent

Sexual harassment, including sexual advances toward three female colleagues. Left Fox News.

James Franco, actor, filmmaker and owner of Studio 4 Acting School

Franco won an award for best actor in his role in *The Disaster Artist* at the Golden Globe awards in early January. Within three days, five women had come forth to accuse him of inappropriate sexual behavior and sexual exploitation, some of them students at his acting school. Some of these women accused him during and after the broadcast on social media and three were interviewed by the Los Angeles Times and an article was published January 11. Franco has continued to appear at award ceremonies (like the National Board of Review gala on January 9) and on television talk shows, awkwardly explaining that he supports the rights of women to call out acts of sexual misconduct, while asserting that his accusers have made inaccurate claims about him. One of his accusers, Violet Paley, feels his public statements rang hollow and seemed self-serving. She feels harassed by his fans for speaking out. During the Golden Globes, Paley was one of several women who took offense at the fact that Franco was wearing a pin supporting Time's Up, an initiative founded by powerful women in the entertainment industry to fight workplace sexual harassment.

Dieter Wedel, film maker and prominent TV director from Germany

Accusations of sexual misconduct are now happening in other countries. Wedel is the first man accused of sexual assault from the German entertainment industry. He is accused not only of sexual assault but rape and attempted rape of actresses over the years beginning in 1980. He has resigned as head of the Bad Hersfeld Theatre Festival. Munich city prosecutors have begun a criminal investigation into sexual assault allegations.

Craig McLachan, Australian actor

Accused of exposure, sexual assault and groping by multiple women on and off stage.

Andy Savage, mega-church pastor, Memphis, Tennessee

Inspired by the #MeToo_anti-sexual harassment movement, 17-year-old Jules Woodson said she decided to send an email to Savage last month with the subject line "Do you remember?" He did not reply.

According to an article (January 7) in Huffpost, she said the incident with Savage occurred in the spring of 1998 when she was a senior in high school. One night, Savage — who was then the youth minister of her church, the Woodlands Parkway Baptist Church in Texas — offered to drive her home after a church event, Woodson said, but took a detour without her consent or knowledge to a deserted forested area.

Woodson said that she initially "assumed we were going to get ice cream."

After parking the vehicle, Savage "unzipped his jeans and pulled out his penis," Woodson said. "He asked me to suck it. I was scared and embarrassed, but I did it. I remember feeling that this must mean that Andy loved me. He then asked me to unbutton my shirt. I did. He started touching me over my bra and then lifted my bra up and began touching my breasts."

After about five minutes, Woodson said Savage suddenly jumped out of the vehicle and ran over to her. He fell to his knees and begged her to not tell anyone about what had just happened. "'You can't tell anyone Jules, please. You have to take this to the grave with you,'" she quotes him as saying.

In the days that followed, Woodson said she was consumed by "fear, shame, anger, and hurt." She decided to tell church leaders about the alleged assault, but they engaged "in a cover-up to protect my abuser and the image of the church," she alleged.

According to Woodson, Savage was not immediately punished for his behavior and the church's leadership only took action after she told members of her all-women discipleship group some of what had transpired that night with the youth pastor.

Even then, however, the church never "came out with an official statement addressing what had happened and/or what was being done about it," Woodson said. "Instead, they held a going-away reception for Andy at the church in which he was allowed to simply say that he had made a poor decision and that it was time for him to move on from our church."

In a blog post, Woodson said she had chosen to go public with her story in the hopes of reaching other sexual assault survivors.

"To anyone who has suffered from sexual abuse in the church and the subsequent cover-up and pressure to remain silent, I want you to know that it is not your fault. Most importantly, I want you to know that you are not alone," she said.

Woodson, who said she'd recently filed a report with the National Center for Missing and Exploited Children about the incident, added that it'd taken her two decades to come forward because she'd felt "pressured by the church to be silent."

Steve Wynn, head of Wynn Resorts and Finance Chairman of the Republican National Committee

Multiple reports of decades of sexual misconduct. Resigned.

Casey Affleck, actor

Inappropriate sexual behavior with two women who had settlements from him. Disinvited to present Best Actress award at Academy Awards.

James Tobeck, screenwriter and director

38 women accused him of sexual misconduct. Dropped by his agent.

Dustin Hoffman, actor

Sexual misconduct with decades of sexual misconduct with many women as well as exposing himself to a minor who was a friend of his daughter in 1980 While being interviewd by John Oliver on a talk show on December 4, 2017 which was an anniversary celebration of his 1997 film "Wag The Dog," Oliver confronted Hoffman with no warning about his sexually abusive history. He is accused of sexual misconduct with TV producer, Wendy Gatsiounis, Anna Graham Hunter, Production Assistant, and Kathryn Rossetter, actress, as well as others. Oliver, according to the Washington Post said that Hoffman is experiencing unprecedented condemnation from those around him as a consequence of his sexually abusive actions. He further said that he is very sad about confronting Hoffman and that Hoffman's apologies were half-hearted.

Ben Affleck, actor

Sexual misconduct and sexual harassment. He has owned and apologized for his behavior and has become an advocate for women's rights to be safe from sexual assault. He is donating future profits made from Weinstein projects to independent filmmakers and victims of sexual assaults.

Steven Seagal, actor

Accused of exposure, rape, and groping of decades of sexually abusing many actresses. The Los Angeles Police Department has opened an investigation of rape and assault of two actresses, Regina Simons and Faviola Dadis.

George W. Bush, former US President

Accused of groping actresses while having his picture taken with actresses.

Patrick Meehan, US Representative, Pennsylvania

The *New York Times* recently reported that Mr. Meehan, a member of the House Ethic Committee and married father of three, pursued a female aide. He became hostile when she rejected his advances. She eventually filed a complaint of sexual harassment against Meehan, and began working from home. She then quit. To settle the complaint, tax payers' money of an undisclosed amount was used to pay her off. She signed a confidentiality agreement which is now being investigated. House and Senate legislators have since introduced proposals to ban the use of taxpayer settlements. Meehan is being urged to repay the funds used in his settlement.

Larry Nassar, USA Gymnastics team doctor, and on staff at Michigan State University

Dr. Larry Nassar has been convicted and sentenced to 175 years in prison in a court hearing in Michigan, guilty of sexually abusing at least 265 girls while he was on the medical staff of Michigan State University and providing medical services for the USA Gymnastics teams. He had already been sentenced 60 years for child pornography charges. Some of his victims were as young as 6 years old and for many, their abuse lasted for years. Many of the victims came to the court hearing and confronted him, making it clear how his actions have hurt them. It was been reported that MSU and the USA Gymnastic organization knew about the abuses but that it was covered up. (If one takes all the victims of Jerry Sandusky, Bill Cosby, and Harvey Weinstein and doubles that number—that is how many Nassar victimized.)

USA Gymnastics and the US Olympic Committee have been under fire from some of the biggest names in the sport, including four Olympic gold medalists. The organizations are being accused of trying to keep a lid on the scandal, waiting five weeks to alert the FBI to a girl's complaint, failing to notify Michigan State University that one of its doctors had been accused, and having McKayla Maroney (one of the gold medalists) sign a secrecy agreement as part of a settlement. When she said she wanted to come out publicly they threatened to charge her $100,000 of the settlement if she did. Due to public pressure, they dropped the charge so that McKayla could testify at the trial. The entire Board of USA Gymnastics have resigned under pressure after months of criticism stemming from the sex abuse scandal. Michigan State University now has law suits against them for covering up complaints of sexual abuse over the years. The president of MSU has resigned.

On January 30, 2018, Congress passed a bill that aims to protect young athletes from sexual abuse and regulate governing bodies of amateur sports. The bill was passed to protect amateur athletes from sexual abuse by enforcing mandatory reporting regulations and extending the statue of limitations for child victims. The bill has a three-pronged approach to protecting athletes and regulating governing bodies of amateur athletics:

1. It requires coaches, trainers, and others to report any sexual abuse allegation to the police within a 24-hour period. (Several women said they reported Nassar to MSU representatives as early as 1997.)

2. It extends the statute of limitations up to 10 years after a victim realizes he or she has been abused.

3. The bill limits athletes under the age of 18 from being alone with an adult who is not their parent. (Nassar often abused young girls while he was alone with them during medical visits.)

Lawmakers from both parties have also called for an investigation into USA Gymnastics and the US Olympic Committee. The NCAA also opened an investigation into how MSU handled the Nassar case.

A reader of this book's draft contributed the following regarding the Nassar case.

"Randall Margraves, I salute you. If only each and every one of us felt the level of outrage, anger, and contempt toward sexual predators as Randall Margraves demonstrated in the following incident (February, 2018):

A father of three victims tried to attack Larry Nassar in a Michigan courtroom on Friday after a judge declined his request for a few minutes alone in a locked room with the 'demon' former sports doctor. He was blocked by an attorney and tackled by sheriff's deputies.

Two of the man's daughters had just told the judge that they and another sister had been sexually abused by Nassar under the guise of medical treatment. Their father, Randall Margraves, told the judge he was a 'distraught father.'

Margraves then looked at Nassar, shook his head and called him a profanity while speaking at the courtroom podium. Margraves then asked for 'five minutes' alone with Nassar. The judge said she couldn't allow that. He asked for one minute, and she again declined.

Margraves then lunged at Nassar, who was sitting nearby.

Margraves was restrained by sheriff's deputies and hauled out of court. He returned a few hours later to apologize to Judge Janice Cunningham, who said there was 'no way' she would punish him under her contempt of court powers. She noted the anguish felt by families over Nassar's crimes."

February, 2018

Wayne Pacelle, CEO of the Humane Society

Sexually harassing women staff. Has resigned..

John Kenneally, Vice President of Monster Energy Company

Sexual harassment of two women on staff. Forced resignation

Vincent Cirrincione, Hollywood talent manager of up-and-coming actresses.

Sexual misconduct of nine "women of color" (Washington Post, 2/2/18). His company has been closed and many of the actresses he managed have cut ties with him, including Halle Barry.

Charlie Walk, music executive and co-host of *The Four*

Sexual misconduct of staff. Put on leave from Variety Records while investigation continues by Fox. Tristan Coppersmith claims she was paid to not tell anyone about sexual misconduct with her.

Burns Strider, senior campaign manager for Hilary Clinton

Sexual misconduct and harassment of a young staffer. He was initially docked pay and told to seek counseling, but was later fired from a campaign group after again being accused of harassment.

Robert Moore, Managing Editor of the New York Daily News

Sexual harassment. Was fired

Alexander "Doc" Jones, Sunday Editor of the NY Daily News

Sexual harassment of several employees. Was fired.

Dyland Howard, senior editor of the *Inquirer* magazine

Told employees about his penis, forced them to listen to pornographic material, talked about their sex lives. Was fired.

Don Johnson, Kentucky State Rep

Sexual harassment. Committed suicide.

Brandon Hixson, Idaho State Representative

Under investigation when he committed suicide.

Woody Allen, actor, director, producer

Allen's adopted daughter, Dylan Farrow, accused her father of sexually abusing her as child. Allen is being shunned by many people in Hollywood.

Paul Haggis, Oscar-winning filmmaker

When Haleigh Breest, a publicist, filed a civil law suit against Mr. Haggis for raping her, three other women were prompted to come forward with their sexual abuse allegations. One of them alleges that Mr. Haggis also raped her. The four women report that they were assaulted in the period from 1996 to 2015. The three other women do not want their names revealed. Mr. Haggis has reseigned as Chair of the Board of the charity he founded, Artists for Peace and Justice.

Scott Baio, actor, television director

Nicole Eggert, who worked with Baio in the sit-com *Charles In Charge* from 1984-1990, filed a police report with the Los Angeles Police Department on 2/7/18 for Baio sexually abusing her as a minor from the time she was 14 to the time she was 17. Alexander Polinsky, who was also a minor during the time of the show, has also come forth with allegations at Mr. Baio also sexually assaulted him. He denies it.

Paul Marciano, co-founder of Guess and CCO (E-News article 2/8/18)

Accused by Kate Upton, a model, of groping, being sexually suggestive. Has resigned. A special committee of Guess is investigating.

Ed Crane, Libertarian leader and ex-president of Cato Company

Sexual harassment of three women plus five others are saying he talked about sex in the office. In 2012, he settled a sexual harassment suit (Politico report of 2/8/18).

Jeff Franklin, producer of Netflix's *Fuller House.*

Warner Brothers fired him for making comments about his sex life and for verbal abuse of staff.

Justin Forsyth, CEO of Save the Children, former Deputy Executive Director, UNICEF

Sexual misconduct. Was fired.

Ryan Seacrest, TV and radio host

Suzie Hardy, hair stylist, accused him of sexual misconduct with her for many years. She lost her job in 2013 when she reported sexual harassment. Investigation continues.

Patrick Demarchelier, famed photographer in the fashion industry

Sexual abuse of those he photographed. Has been fired as photographer for Glamour, Vogue, and Vanity Fair magazines.

Christina Garcia, California Assemblywoman

Groping two male staff members and making lewd sexual suggestions

Is under investigation

Autumn Burke, California Assemblywoman

Talking about anal sex with staff, has apologized and taken responsibility.

Is under investigation.

March, 2018

Tony Tooke, head of US Forest Service

Accused of multiple sexual relationships with subordinates during his 40-year career before he became Chief. Resigned March 7, 2018, effective immediately.

John Asher, Society of Children's Book Writers and Illustrators

> Expelled. The Oklahoma Writers' Federation cancelled him from making the keynote address in May, 2018.

There are many more accusations to come in the future. It is important to remember that sexual assault is motivated by hostility, power, and control. Sexual assaults are not motivated by sexual desire. Many of those accused have accumulated power and feel they can use it to control and overpower others, especially women. As the movement continues, a great many of us who have been over-powered will now feel empowered.

IMPORTANT EVENTS: "ME TOO" AND "TIMES UP" MOVEMENTS

Time Magazine Award for Person of the Year- December 18, 2017

Time magazine gave person of the year to a group of women named "The Silence Breakers." This group of women represents the people who came forward to report sexual misconduct. Their voices launched the "Me, Too" movement. According to the article "these silence breakers have started a revolution of refusal, gathering strength by the day, and in the past two months alone, their collective anger has spurred immediate and shocking results: nearly every day, CEO's have been fired, moguls toppled, icons disgraced. In some cases, criminal charges have been brought."

The "silence breakers" include:

1. Susan Fowler, Engineer at Uber, alleged pervasive sexism and sexual harassment at Uber workplace in February, 2017. Twenty employees were fired.

2. Taylor Swift, singer, pop superstar. In August, 2017, she won a court case against a former radio host she accused of groping her in 2013. Her testimony was widely covered.

3. Ashley Judd, actress, accused Harry Weinstein of sexual misconduct.

4. Adama Iwu, a corporate lobbyist and activist, was highlighted in the *Time* article for her courage to organize more than 147 women to expose sexual harassment in California Government. After experiencing sexual harassment herself, Iwu was shocked at the lack of response that was given to her by those who witnessed the

groping assault. Instead of ignoring what happened to her, Iwu decided to take action against those men who were accustomed to sexually harassing women without any consequences, *Le Monde*, a French daily newspaper, reported.

5. A fifth woman, using the pseudonym Isabel Pascual, is a strawberry picker who was harassed by a man who threatened her and her children, the magazine said.

Since the *Time* award and story in December, 2017, many, many people have reported their sexual harassment and sexual misconduct.

THE GOLDEN GLOBES AWARDS, January 7, 2018

The 75th Golden Globes was dominated by powerful speeches about sexual abuse following the Weinstein revelations last year. Many celebrities wore black to stand in solidarity with victims of sexual harassment.

The night was focused on campaigns like #MeToo and Time's Up, the latter of which was a project launched by more than 300 actresses, writers and directors. It is a legal fund set up for sexual harassment victims.

One of the most memorable parts of the evening was a talk by Oprah Winfrey. "A new day is on the horizon. Speaking your truth is the most powerful tool we all have. For too long women have not been believed or heard if they dare speak the truth to the power of these men. But time is up. Their time is up!"

GRAMMY AWARDS January 28, 2018

At the Grammy Award program, dozens of artists and music industry players sported white roses in support of the Time's Up and #MeToo movements against sexual abuse and harassment.

ACADEMY AWARDS March 4, 2018

Jimmy Kimmel said in his monologue opening the Oscars "This is history happening right here." This was the first Academy Awards, since the New York Times exposé on producer Harvey Weinstein, the first since "Times Up," the first since #Me Too became a household name across America. The Golden Globes had set the bar relatively high for awards shows when it came to addressing the issue of sexual misconduct in Hollywood, and one of the biggest questions going into the Oscars was how the biggest show of the season would handle the biggest story in Hollywood. It did include clear and specific calls for change, most of them by women, which could lead in the long run to a more equitable entertainment industry for everyone.

The #MeToo movement against sexual harassment was saluted several ways at the Academy Awards. A segment dedicated to the issue was narrated by Ashley Judd, Salma Hayek, and Annabella Sciorra, three of the dozens of women who have accused Hollywood mogul Harvey Weinstein of sexual misconduct, helping touch off the #MeToo movement.

Judd said, "The changes we are witnessing are being driven by the powerful sound of new voices, of different voices, of our voices, joining together in a mighty chorus that is finally saying: Times Up!"

Times Up was launched on January 1, 2018 and is a legal defense fund that aims to support people reporting sexual harassment in the entertainment industry and beyond. Judd also said "Those of us who have come forward, we've often been disbelieved, minimized, shamed and so much of the movement is about externalizing that shame and putting it back where it belongs, which is with the perpetrator."

Hayek said, "So we salute those unstoppable spirits who kicked ass and broke through the biased perceptions of their race, their genders and their ethnicities."

Sciorra added, "And on this ninetieth anniversary evening, when the Oscars celebrates its timeless classics, we look forward as well"

Frances McDormand's acceptance speech for the Best Actress Award included a rousing call to arms to the entertainment industry. Her voice breaking, she invited all the evening's female nominees—"the actors…the filmmakers, the producers, the directors, the writers, the cinematographers, the composers, the songwriters, the designers"—to stand up. Then she issued a challenge: "Look around, ladies and gentlemen, because we all have stories to tell and projects we need financed. Don't talk to us about it at the parties tonight; invite us into your office in a couple days…or you can come to ours, and we'll tell you all about them"

"I have two words to leave with you tonight," she continued, "inclusion rider."

A rider is a part of a contract: by insisting on an inclusion rider, a powerful Hollywood player could ensure that the project they are signing on for will include a more gender and race inclusive talent pool. She had primed the audience to expect words about Times Up or #MeToo, and what she gave them instead was a suggestion that could lead to real money for people of color, women of all races, and other under-represented groups in Hollywood.

Traditionally, the previous year's winner for best actor presents the award for best actress. But Casey Affleck, who settled two sexual harassment lawsuits in 2010, did not participate in this year's ceremony. James Franco, who was an early favorite to be nominated in the best-actor category before accusation of sexual misconduct arose, losing him the votes of at least some of the Academy, was a no-show.

ROYAL FOUNDATION FORUM

The first Royal Foundation Forum, is a philanthropic organization currently run by Meghan Markle, Prince Harry, Prince William and Kate Middleton, according to ABC News. The first engagement of the royal couples was held in London, England on February 28, 2018. They spoke of various causes close to their hearts at the forum. Two of the causes are #Me Too and Times Up. Meghan Markle is a long time supporter of women's and girl's rights and stressed how important is to strengthen campaigns like Times Up and #Me Too. She feels that men and women must come together to support these movements. She said "Women don't need to find a voice…they have a voice. They need to feel empowered to use it, and people need to be encouraged to listen. There is no better time than to really continue to shine a light on women feeling empowered and people really helping to support them, men included. It makes such a tremendous difference."

Markle also hinted she is already working behind the scenes, though she said her efforts will really get going after her royal wedding to Prince Harry in May. "I guess we will wait a couple of months and then we can hit the ground running." Meanwhile, Harry heaped praise on his future bride, adding "I am personally incredibly proud and excited that my soon-to-be wife, who is equally passionate about seeing positive change in the world, will soon be joining us with this work."

SEXUAL MISCONDUCT SPURS NEW ELECTIONS

According to a Wikipedia report on March 28, 2018, there have been allegations accusing 41 persons of sexual misconduct, including sexual harassment and sexual assault. There was one person from the Executive Branch (Donald Trump), one from the United States Senate (Al Franken), seven from the United States House of Representatives (John Conyers, Blade Farenthold, Trent Franks, Alcee Hastings, Ruben Kihuen, Eric Massa and Pat Meehan) and one Federal Judge(Alex Kozinski). The rest are State politicians. Because of all the resignations, firings, and retirements, there are many, many special elections that will be held in 2018 to fill vacancies left by lawmakers accused of sexual misconduct.

BACKLASH

As dozens of women came forward to accuse not only Nassar but also a large number of men, some of these survivors are being attacked in the social media. Amanda Miller, Chairman of the Sociology Department at the University of Indianapolis, wrote in a report for Fox 59 news in Indianapolis about the "Me,Too" movement on January 17, 2018: "The viral campaign shines a light on the widespread issue of sexual assault and harassment of women, especially in the workplace." She commends all the brave women who have come forward with their own stories of sexual abuse as a result of the movement, which has sparked a feminist social movement. She writes that "…amongst the heart-wrenching accounts of sexual abuse are comments from the public blaming and shaming the survivors. This backlash could stop others from coming forward with their own accounts of the sexual assault." She quotes a woman who has been sexually assaulted as saying "we are really worried about people not believing us. That gives us a reluctance to come forward, but then if we come forward and instantly the reaction from people is that it cannot be true…it discourages you from sharing your story."

Catherine Deneuve and several women had an open letter published in *Le Monde*, a French daily newspaper, stating they felt that men were being unfairly targeted by sexual misconduct allegations. She has since backed down from this position to fully support those who have been sexually abused.

In our culture, unfortunately, there are those who blame the victim. One reason people blame a victim is to distance themselves from an unpleasant occurrence and thereby confirm their own invulnerability to the risk. By labeling or accusing the victim, others can see the victim as different from themselves. People reassure themselves by thinking *Because I am not like her, because I do not do that, this would never happen to me.* Or, *she went to his hotel room, what did she expect?*

"Men like to tease by pinching us on the butt or making sexual suggestions"; "you just have to put up with a boss who is doing and saying sexual stuff"; "all this about men doing sexual things to women, what is the big deal?" Believe me, I have heard it all while writing this book. In essence, women are sometimes being blamed for their own abuse.

Now there are those vocal people who are discrediting the whole Me, Too movement and think we are all over-reacting. That is what is being referred to as the "backlash." There is a big difference between those situations where there is friendly flirting and touching among friends. That is very much different than a person sexually harassing or sexually assaulting an unwilling person in the workplace.

The idea that so many people are turning a blind eye to the prevalence of sexual abuse, or worse, helping to support its continuation by not taking a stand to speak up or fight against it, reveals a societal problem that we can no longer ignore.

CHAPTER 3

WAKE UP AND FIGHT

"I had no idea that my boss's groping my ass as he walked by was 'sexual abuse.' Somehow in my upbringing I had gotten the idea that this was more or less normal behavior, and it just meant he liked me. It made me feel I had job security," said Marilyn, a 28-year-old administrative assistant.

Harmless teasing? No. Marilyn's boss showed no respect for appropriate boundaries. In all likelihood, he was oblivious to, ignoring, or intentionally crossing sex and intimacy boundaries with others, as well. The more "practice" he got at using his position of power to do as he pleased, unchallenged, the more ingrained his objectification of women became. Also, the more he got away with exploiting women, the more susceptible he became to acting out in more and more egregious ways. The boss in this case was recently arrested for his participation in a sex trafficking ring, a "side business" that had netted him many thousands of dollars at the horrifying expense of others.

Some have the notion that Me, Too is about coming out in public, telling on men like Marilyn's boss for sexual harassment. That is happening every day, as noted in Chapter 2, as people are calling out well-known, high profile people, many names we know from Hollywood or Washington, DC.

But Me, Too is not just a swell of people coming forward; it is growing into a tsunami of truth-telling—everything from finally voicing 40-year-old incest incidents to speaking up as the sixth or seventh person to accuse a celebrity, adding validation to the victims.

Because of my extensive background, I know about things I honestly wish I didn't know about; I know what it feels like to not want to see the abuse, depravity, and evil in our midst. But you know what? Now, more than ever in history, awareness is very, very important, because it fuels the will of the people (us) who can stop and prevent abuse. We are not powerless, we simply need to have the courage, organization, and resolve to fix this global problem, starting in our own home, town, and country.

THE SOROPTIMIST ORGANIZATION

Soroptimist is an organization of business and professional women working to improve the lives of women and girls in local communities throughout the world. The name, "soroptimist," means "best for women." Members undertake a number of projects that help educate potential victims of sex trafficking and also helps women and girls who have escaped from sex trafficking. Often counseling and shelters are provided by various chapters. There are nearly 75 thousand members in 120 countries and territories.

The organization is active in getting legislation passed against sex traffickers. One of their best programs is to give girls and women economic roles and skills to achieve financial empowerment and independence, and also provide victims with living and educational skills. You can make a difference by becoming a member. Visit their web site, www.soroptimist.org.

Soroptimist Vision & Mission
(Source: Official web site, www.soroptimist.org)

VISION
Women and girls have the resources and opportunities to reach their full potential and live their dreams.

MISSION
Soroptimist improves the lives of women and girls through programs leading to social and economic empowerment.

CORE VALUES
Soroptimist International of the Americas is committed to:

Gender Equality: Women and girls live free from discrimination.

Empowerment: Women and girls are free to act in their own best interest.

Education: Women and girls deserve to lead full and productive lives through access to education.

Diversity & Fellowship: Women from varied backgrounds and perspectives work together to improve the lives of women and girls.

It is estimated that 300,000 children each year are recruited or kidnapped into the sex trade. Our society does not seem to want to know this because it really is beyond what anyone wants to realize. It is estimated that the average age of children who join are 12 years old. That is heartbreaking, isn't it? They should be going to school, going to movies with friends, and just generally being happy kids. Instead they are being raped over and over, sometimes by many men in the same day. It is beyond my imagination. What is horrifying is that some parents or other family members have sold their children to these organizations for money and drugs. Some estimates are that child trafficking is a 31 million dollar industry worldwide and is on the rise in the U.S.

The victims of sexual trafficking are kids who are running away, or they could be your innocent child from a good home. That is why education about predators is so very necessary.

Dr Katarina Rosenblatt, leading expert in human trafficking and author of the book, *Stolen: The True Story of a Sex Trafficking Survivor* was herself a victim of the child sex industry. "I was recruited in my middle school at 14, falling for a false friend who invited me for a sleepover party," Rosenblatt writes. "My classmate's father was a pedophile and trafficker using his own daughter to recruit other youngsters. Selling us, he had an older man kidnap, blindfold, and transport us to an apartment being used as a brothel...I became very addicted to drugs...which left me with yet another vulnerability to being recruited a third time at 15 in the apartment building where I lived. This time, it was an older father-figure type preying upon my need for love and protection. In total, I was a victim from age 12 to 17, off and on. The day-to-day was mostly a blur hoping to find 'love' in the eyes of the traffickers or customers who paid the trafficker to be with us either through drugs or money."

Even if a girl escapes, as you can imagine, she is scarred forever. Thankfully there are organizations and therapists who help mend the victims' hearts and minds. My friend who donates generously to the Soroptimists said, "I can make more of a difference if I help those who are helping so many girls and women."

Teen girls are especially susceptible to recruitment if they do not have a stable family nor their natural craving for love fulfilled. Rosenblatt shares, "I fell for the false love and false attention of the men that came, never staying and always breaking my heart, leaving me confused and lonely even more than before. To them it was a game or a fantasy, but to me it was a sad string of disappointment experiences controlled by dangerous men who carried guns and used intimidation to keep us controlled by drugs and threats. It reality these traffickers are men who cared nothing for me or my friends."

Another organization to be aware of is Bridging Freedom (www.bridgingfreedom.org). According to their web site, around 300,000 children are prostituted against their will each year in the US. The nonprofit group states:

"Bridging Freedom's mission is to combat minor sex-trafficking by bringing restoration to those rescued and victim prevention to those we reach with our message. We educate the community and work with partnering organizations to increase awareness about this horrendous issue. We are also working to build Florida's urgently needed therapeutic safe home campus community to provide long-term, comprehensive care to these victims in a secure environment. We are in the building and development phases and are gaining progressive momentum toward realizing our goal of providing this urgently needed healing solution."

Also check out the nonprofit's web site www.polarisproject.org. Polaris is a leader in the global fight to eradicate modern slavery of all types. Named after the North Star that guided slaves to freedom in the US, Polaris systemically disrupts the human trafficking networks that rob human beings of their lives and their freedom.

In December 2007, Polaris launched the National Human Trafficking Hotline, which victims and survivors can call to be connected with advocates who offer support and services to get help and stay safe. Between then and December 2016, the organization fielded 32,208 potential cases of human trafficking.

"KIDDIE PORN" RINGS

Many children as young as three or even younger are used to perform in "kiddie porn" films and magazines. This is not the warped interest of a few perverts: Obviously, there are a lot of adults out in the world who pay money to keep this widespread, exploitive industry financially profitable. Some people claim that viewing pornography is a "victimless crime." It is incomprehensible that anyone could consider these children "victimless." Very often the victims of this kind of abuse grow up to feel used and like "damaged goods". They may feel they are only worthy of being exploited and may exploit others sexually as adults in an effort to regain a sense of power and control. Self-esteem can be damaged and serious other problems such as drug addiction, aggressiveness, and mal-adjustment to life are just some of the repercussions.

CULTS

Tragically, children are being sexually abused in various cults across the nation. Members of those cults are isolated from society and have been taught to obey their leaders blindly. The children of these cult members often do not receive education or medical care, nor are births or deaths recorded. The children are trained to control their feelings, not show emotion, and, above all, to be obedient.

In some cults, the children are sexually abused as a matter of course. For instance, one cult trained its female children to be "happy hookers for Jesus." Adult/child sexual relationships and incest were encouraged and venereal disease among the children was rampant.

Some cult leaders are looked upon as "godly" and thereby entitled to whatever they want, including sexual access to children.

A woman who escaped a cult said that she had not minded the leader demanding her obedience and sexual favors, but when he expected the same from their five-year-old daughter, she was appalled and found a way to get herself and daughter out of the abusive, prison-like existence. Educating young women on the far-reaching ramifications of joining a cult is critical, not only to save their lives but to protect against innocent children being born into a cult.

PERPETRATORS IN POSITIONS OF TRUST

Children are the sweet honey that draws the evil flies to wherever they are. Perpetrators are found in churches, Girl and Boy Scout clubs, the YMCA, and other youth organizations, teachers, day care centers, and in every circumstance where children are involved. Even highly educated individuals such as doctors, lawyers, and other professionals who are in influential positions in society and, thus, may be somewhat protected by their respectability, have perpetrators in their midst. The doctors also have especially easy access to children in their practices. Children have a high degree of vulnerability to "respectable" perpetrators because both the child and his parents trust the perpetrator. The child's safety is, therefore, high risk because his guard is down, as is that of his parents. These respectable people are powerful; frequently they are not prosecuted when it is discovered they are victimizing children because of their influence. Parents must be aware that perpetrators come from all socio-economic classes if they are to protect vulnerable children.

Some perpetrators purposely are involved in professions and in voluntary positions in which there are children so that they may have easy access to sexually abusing children. They may offer babysitting services, or take jobs and participate in community events that involve children. Not that every ice-cream truck driver is a child molester, but I personally know several women who were childhood victims of the neighborhood vendor who easily enticed any child he chose to "try the new flavor" inside the truck or van.

Perpetrators attend sporting events for children and/or volunteer to coach children's sports, offer to chaperone overnight trips, loiter in places children frequent, such as playgrounds, malls and game arcades. A friend told me that she and two girlfriends were dropped off at a movie theatre by their parents and an adult male preyed on the girls by sitting next to them and masturbating. They were so upset and scared they were frozen in their seats. The man left before the movie ended; the girls never told their parents. Think about that—even when an incident is so obviously not the child's fault such as with this stranger in a cinema, children are often reluctant to speak up. This is where education can be so important, i.e., teaching children when and how to tell a responsible adult when something happens that makes them feel uncomfortable or scared.

The Catholic Church

All churches have a leadership hierarchy, people in positions of authority who can use their position and influence with church members and the local community in constructive or destructive ways. In recent years, the Catholic Church has come under national and international scrutiny for the extensive and systemic problem of child sexual abuse within the Church, as well as the Church's decision to ignore and often conceal the truth about the crimes of serial sexual predators in their churches and schools. It's about time.

For many years the Catholic Church was aware that its priests and nuns were sexually abusing children, although it was covered up. In a document issued in 1962, the Vatican instructed Catholic bishops around the world to cover up cases of sexual abuse or risk being thrown out of the Church, according to an article in *The Guardian* in 2003. Its sister newspaper, *The Observer*, obtained the 40-year-old confidential document from the secret Vatican archives in 2003. Lawyers called the document a "blueprint for deception and concealment." One British lawyer acting for the Church child abuse victims had described it as "explosive." The document was a 69-page Latin document bearing the seal of Pope John XXIII and was sent to every bishop in the world. The instructions outline a policy of "strictest" secrecy in dealing with allegations of sexual abuse and threatens those who speak out with excommunication.

When a particular diocese found out one of its priests was a predator, that priest would be assigned to another diocese. One of my clients was abused by a priest who was transferred out to another church where he was made the director of the youth program! (He has graciously shared more of his story in the Foreword of this book.)

Concealment and reassignment of pedophile clergy members has continued to surface and the children within the Church continue to be victimized. The abuse not only occurs in the individual dioceses but also in other Catholic orders including the Christian Brothers, Jesuits, the Franciscans and many more orders, according to *The Guardian*. According to Wikipedia, priests in these Orders are distinctly different than parish priests who are under diocesan control. They answer to no one except the Vatican and they find it easier to hide sexual abuse and go undetected. Not only do they also transfer priests like the dioceses do, they also have Orders all over the world where they can hide a predator priest. These Orders have increased availability of children to sexually abuse because they staff hospitals, boarding schools, seminaries, and schools. National Public Radio (NPR) reports that 1/3 of Catholic clergies serve in religious orders. For instance, Jesuits teach in high schools and Franciscans serve the poor. According to *The Guardian*, 11 men were sexually abused by priests assigned to teach them while training to be priests in the Mirfield Yorkshire Seminary in England. All 11 have settled their claims of sexual abuse with the Catholic order that ran it. Furthermore, NPR reports that the Jesuits settled with more than 110 Eskimos in Alaska for 50 million dollars. *Newsweek* reports that the Catholic Church has a long history of protecting highly placed Catholic leaders from charges of sexual abuse. When reports surfaced in 1995 that Austrian Cardinal Hans Hermann Groer had molested monks and school boys, the sexual abuse was dismissed by Bishop Kurt Krenn as "boyish pranks." There were also claims that victims were paid "hush money" to buy their silence. The allegations of sexual abuse against Cardinal Groer proved to be true.

The victims are often unwilling to report their abuse for many years because the perpetrators hold positions of sacred trust. The victims may be confused or unable to comprehend that what is happening to them is "sexual abuse." The priest may threaten them or make them fearful that if they do tell someone they will not be believed. Sometimes children are told that the abuse is part of a religious ritual. The guilt, shame, and fear of the childhood sexual abuse often continues long into adulthood.

I provided therapy for over a year to one of the Church's victims named John. He gave me permission to share his story here, and also he talks about it in the Foreword he wrote for this book. Like I am, he is committed to getting more eye-opening information in the hands of as many people as possible and hopes to impact the growing movement of effective prevention.

John's sexual abuse by a priest began the summer before he was to start attending the parish high school. Father Bob was a new priest who everyone liked, including John's family who welcomed him warmly into their lives and home. The first incident of abuse was when John was 13 and was invited by Father Bob to accompany him to a neighboring state to visit a parish family. The priest performed oral sex on him in their shared bedroom, telling John that it was okay to show love for each other and that God accepted and encouraged it. John felt responsible for the abuse and was nauseated. He had no idea what to do and it never occurred to him to tell anyone what had happened.

That was the beginning of seven years of abuse. Father Bob was an expert at making John feel special and completely dependent on him. Paradoxically, John was both terrified of him and yet he lived for his approval. Because Father Bob was a priest, John felt he had no choice except to comply. (If you did not grow up in a Catholic family, it may be hard for you to comprehend the enormous amount of power that church leaders are imbued with and that this is embraced by the trusting parishioners.) Father Bob used his considerable influence over John while convincing him that any resistance to the abuse by his priest meant that the boy was a bad person. They took frequent trips together and spent time in his room at the rectory. They drank a lot of alcohol together and John used the alcohol to cope.

John felt like he was becoming two people—one who did well in school and had a lot of friends, and one who he loathed, as he was required to visit Father Bob in his room. Upon graduation, John began attending a well-known prestigious Catholic College out of state, partly to get away from Father Bob. But the predatory priest visited John frequently despite John's efforts to keep him away. He was able to limit the visits somewhat which made Father Bob very angry. Then Father Bob got a position at the college to be an assistant rector there at the graduate school. After he arrived, anytime John would resist him, Father Bob would either become a raging, threatening Father Bob, or a tearful, pitiful Father Bob. At age 20, John finally was able to break off from him.

He moved back home after graduation and began to realize how the sexual abuse had deeply affected his life. He was depressed, had relationship issues, felt angry all the time and had a drinking problem. He felt he had hit bottom and had no hope, and nothing to lose, so he contacted the bishop where Father Bob was a priest and told him about Father Bob's abuse. The bishop was placating, at best, but did nothing and did not want to hear that Father Bob probably was still abusing children. John had hoped that at least his warning could save other children from the agony he was in. The bishop moved Father Bob from parish to parish for the next nine years.

Even though John had contacted the bishop about Father Bob's abuse, feeling a moral obligation to protect other children from the same fate he experienced, the Church, ironically, felt no such moral obligation to protect children nor act accordingly. In 1998, John decided that the only way he would get the diocese to take action against Father Bob was to expose his abuse publicly. Before he did so, he knew he had to tell his parents and brothers. Up until then, only a few people in his life knew what had happened to him. Both his parents were, and are, active committed Catholics. They were devastated, angry, and confused. But they supported him as did his brothers.

His first attempt to "go public" and expose the abuse involved speaking to a reporter at *Newsday*, Long Island's most widely read newspaper.

The paper would not publish the story because they seemed to minimize John's experiences. Finally, he decided that the only way to remove the priest was to take direct action. He wrote an open letter to the parishioners of the parish in which Father Bob served, telling them of his abuse and their bishop's knowledge of it for nine years. His father and two brothers and John stood outside his church on a Sunday morning in July, 1989, and handed copies of the letter to people as they left Mass. He had called the television news outlets and NBC had a camera crew and reporter at the church. They captured the near riot that ensued as parishioners yelled at them to leave the church grounds. Parishioners attacked the cameraman, injuring him and tried to grab the microphone from the reporter. The dramatic story was the lead for both the 6 and 11 o'clock news that evening in New York. The diocese issued a meaningless statement. But the priest was at last removed from the Church.

When John went public, he did not know how his revelations would affect his relationships with family and friends, his work, and every aspect of his life. I respect John so much for doing what he had to do regardless of the consequence for him. He indeed showed great courage and added so much light to a secret dark area of the Church. The Church never offered an apology, therapy, or any recognition of what had happened. He still feels an ethical and personal responsibility to help other survivors and to try to hold the church accountable. He works closely with other victims on a volunteer basis and with groups which are helping survivors. He walks his talk and is a gift to those who have also shared his experiences.

Even though the sexual abuse has affected his adult life, he has grown and healed much of his trauma. He has a loving marriage and family with two children, and is a successful business owner. John is an advocate for others who have been sexually abused by priests and personally meets with and helps them.

The Catholic Church is attempting to right some of its wrongs. In December of 2017, Pope Frances issued a document that tells bishops around the world that they must practice "zero tolerance" for clergy who sexually abuse children. In the letter sent to all the bishops on December, 28, 2017, he writes "I would like us to renew our complete commitment to insure that the atrocities will no longer take place in our midst" There is hope for the future, although the issue of sexual abuse in the Catholic Church of such magnitude will not be solved merely by a letter anytime in the future. This issue is so deeply ingrained within the Church and so pervasive that it is unlikely to be resolved anytime in the near future. John feels the bishops and cardinals who shielded, supported, and protected the abusive priests in the midst need to acknowledge their actions and have the integrity and courage to step aside. The people who step into their shoes need to reach out to the survivors of abuse, welcome them into the church and find out what they can do to help them. They need to proactively inquire into the spiritual and emotional health of the survivors and their families. They need to do whatever it takes to get them well through therapy and support in their parishes. Let every member of their diocese know the names of the priests who have abused children and try to find out if there are other victims of those priests who have not yet come forward. They need to invite victims of abuse to come to their churches, to speak to the parishioners about their experiences. They need to stop paring words, splitting hairs and listening to their lawyers. They need to settle their lawsuits with victims fairly and quickly.

John said, "If the church had done these things when the victims of abuse had first come forward, it would have avoided millions of dollars worth of lawsuits. Its bishops and cardinals would also be sleeping better at night and its good and holy priests, who are a legion, would not be so embarrassed to be priests in the Roman Catholic Church. It would still have the voice of moral authority and credibility in America. And people like me, who went to them for help, could say to ourselves, I was abused, which was awful, but I was saved and nurtured by my church when I came forward.'"

Other Churches

Clergy, church leaders, and religious institutions generally exist to offer spiritual and moral guidance and a healthy community for those faithful followers under their protection. Unfortunately, systemic problems of child sexual abuse by trusted leaders in churches and religious organizations goes beyond the Catholic Church. Abuse by clergy of many different faiths is well-documented. The betrayal of trust that the victims experience when they are sexually abused by clergy is very painful. Abusers manipulate the victims' trust and reverence for the clergy as well as the church in order to coerce them into sex. Victims then are left with feelings of shame, confusion, and anger. The victim is betrayed not only by the abuser, but also by the religious institution that allowed the abuse to occur through the manipulation of trust and faith. Many churches insist on handling allegations of sexual abuse internally and strongly discourage intervention by outside authorities because they are an insular religious community. The abuse is not reported and the perpetrator my continue abusing or, if he leaves the church, he probably will continue his abuse elsewhere.

Foster Home and Group Home Abuse

Thousands of children and adolescents across the United States are in foster and group homes. The children are removed from their homes for abuse, neglect and other reasons, and are placed into care in other homes. The homes are supposed to provide a safe haven for emotionally distressed children removed from dangerous environments.

Unfortunately, too often these children are subjected to further trauma, neglect, and abuse by the very people who are foster parents. They take children in to sexually abuse them, although the surrogate care providers and agencies are responsible for facilitating a loving and safe environment. Within these settings, sexual predators may take advantage to groom and abuse vulnerable children. Without any family, trusted adults, or diligent advocates to speak up for them, these children are forced to endure neglect and sexual, physical, or emotional abuse for many years in silence. Victims are coerced into remaining in a dangerous situation, fearing further abuse or other repercussions if they report the abuse.

For example, one 14-year-old girl was told by her male foster parent (along with his complicit wife), "If you leave here, you will be living on the street. You'll have to be a prostitute for strangers, and you will never have a home or friends. Is that what you want?"

Those who are responsible for the children's safety, such as social workers, school teachers, and others who come into contact with them must learn to detect sexual abuse signs so that these desperate children can be helped. Any child, male or female, in foster care should be closely monitored. Fortunately, the majority of foster and group homes are loving, protective, and nurturing. The children are safer and better off than they were at the home they came from. Thus, foster parents can be a child's savior from sexual abuse, although sometimes the perpetrators. Determining the truth of the situation is our responsibility as a society, a job we entrust to government social agencies. "Child Protective Services" (CPS) is the name of a government agency in many states responsible for providing child protection, which includes responding to reports of child abuse or neglect. Some states use other names, often attempting to reflect more family-centered (as opposed to child-centered) practices, such as "Department of Children & Family Services" (DCFS). CPS is also known by the name of "Department of Social Services" (DSS) or simply "Social Services."

Boy Scouts and Other Youth Organizations

The BSA is one of the largest youth organizations in the United States with 2.7 million members and over one million adult volunteers. While many boys have good experiences in scouting, many others do not. Unfortunately, the BSA has a well-documented 100-year-old problem with child sexual abuse. By 1920, the BSA had already established a "red flag" system used to identify adult volunteers who were known to sexually molest scouts. These volunteers were put on probation, but that did nothing to prevent predators from having access to Boy Scouts. Throughout the years, the BSA has undertaken steps to improve child abuse prevention policies, ensuring greater protection of minor scouts. In 2010, a scout was molested by a Scout Master in Portland Oregon. The trial lasted six weeks and garnered international press coverage, ultimately resulting in a jury award to the victim of compensatory and punitive damages which totaled near twenty million dollars! Many victims of sexual abuse by leaders in institutions have been awarded big settlements, which certainly encourages the organizations to protect their members. There are many cases of sex abuse allegations leading to lawsuits against BSA in the 1970's and 1980's in the courts at this time. It is not unusual for victims of sexual abuse to wait many years to reveal the crimes committed against them, especially for males, who typically feel great shame from their experience with their scout leaders.

Will the culture of Scouts change due to the new 2018 policy? From Cub Scout to Eagle Scout, the Boy Scouts of America will now admit girls into every level of their Scouting program. I would like to think that leadership and parents of both boys and girls will be even more vigilant in screening the adults who have influence and access to the children and teens.

Teachers

It has been estimated that about 10% of students suffer some form of sexual abuse during their school careers. Abusive acts include lewd comments, exposing children to pornography, inappropriate conversation (texting or sexting), peeping in the locker room, and sexual touching or grabbing. In widely reported news stories, we see that in school settings more than other institutions, perpetrators are not only men, but women teachers and substitute teachers. In 2017, a female teacher (age 30) in Oviedo, Florida, was arrested for coercing a 15-year-old girl into sexual activity, multiple times over a two-month period. We read about female teachers who are even married with children of their own who have sex with teenage boys. Psychologically, we now know that this harms the minor emotionally; it is not something the boy feels proud of, as may have been a popular view in past times. It does damage, in varying degrees, to the victim's ability to have healthy, trusting, and/or intimate relationships in the future.

We cannot always count on the very adults we entrust with our children. We must teach each and every child about the dangers of inappropriate actions by adults, even ones we have told them to trust and obey. When something happens, especially coming from a teacher, it is confusing and upsetting for the child and they will not know what to do unless they have been taught to tell a parent or trustworthy adult.

Doctors, Dentists, Mental Health or Other Trusted Professionals

In a medical setting, children and their parents want to trust their doctors, dentists, nurses and others. These perpetrators hold a great deal of power over victims, so much so that victims often fear that no one would believe them if they reported the abuse. According to a report by the Atlanta-Journal Constitution, one Delaware-based pediatrician was recently indicted on 471 charges of molesting, raping and abusing children in 2010, after he drugged patients with lollipops and videotaped his crimes. Some of his victims were just months old. Some children do not realize they have been touched inappropriately and videotaped during the examinations.

The article said that of the 2,400 physicians found guilty of sexually abusing their patients, half are still practicing medicine to this day. Patients may be abused and videotaped while sedated. Be aware if your child seems afraid of a doctor or others and stay in the examining room with them.

Hospitals are not a guaranteed safety zone, either. Sexual predators in these settings can exploit a patient's injuries, limitations, vulnerability or other impaired states in order to commit crimes of sexual violence. Children are particularly vulnerable. Again, those who are responsible for the child need to be aware if any sexual abuse is evident, and I'll emphasize again, all children need to be educated to tell someone if they are being abused.

AM I SAYING SEXUAL ABUSE IS EVERYWHERE?

Yes, I came to that conclusion based on empirical evidence, my direct experience observing and conversing directly with victims, as well as perpetrators, in my decades as a therapist. Every story and example I share in this book is with the purpose of heightening your awareness. So often we can see a situation that fits our idea of potential or actual abuse, but are blind to what is happening right in front of us because we did not have an awareness of what to look for.

What Is Going On Around Me I Should Know About?

PORNOGRAPHY: There are millions of pornographic images of minors being posted, shared and sold on the internet, each one exploiting an innocent child. In a case I know about, a father took photos of his three young daughters while they were nude, forcing them to assume seductive poses. He sold the pictures to a porn ring, as well as taped the pictures on several walls in his house for his friends to enjoy. The mother was absent from the home due to commitment to a psychiatric facility for severe mental problems. He was finally busted when an air conditioning repairman was not entertained by the décor, and told the police.

PROSTITUTION: Yes, there are women, men, girls, and boys who sell sex to strangers or are coerced to perform sexual acts for payment collected by another person (sometimes called their "pimp"). As disturbing as this may be to consider, be aware that if a child suddenly has money (dollars or quarters) that didn't come from their parent or a known source, the girl or boy may be getting paid for sexual activities, and not even realize the depravity of the person bribing them. But there are also people, mainly women and children, who are exploited for commercial sex within their own home and/or family.

Sometimes the victim receives no money, just threats. Jimmy, age 10, had been moved to the home of a relative after his mother abandoned him to run away with her boyfriend. During his stay at an uncle's house, the uncle brought acquaintances home with the promise of oral sex. Jimmy was forced to perform it on them. The uncle collected the money from the "customers" and told Jimmy, "This is the least you can do. After all, you have to earn your keep. If you don't do it, then I will send you away."

EXHIBITIONISM: Exposing a sexual organ for the purpose of arousing or gratifying sexual desire is called exhibitionism, and is a common acting-out behavior of both perpetrators and (later) victims. If you have never been exposed to an exhibitionist (no pun intended), you may not realize how shocking and traumatizing it can be. Because the abuser is not touching the victim in a sexual or hurtful way, they may not be aware just how harmful and abusive this is. At one time in our society the "flasher" was depicted as a man in a trench coat, often as a topic of humor. No more. Exhibitionists should be reported, though that is often easier said, than done.

A woman told me she went up to a librarian in a large public library to report that a man sitting at a nearby table in a work area had been staring at her, which she had ignored until she realized he was masturbating. She was in such a panic she could hardly speak and was mortified to have to describe what had just happened. The librarian left her alone at a desk to go find someone else to tell, and the woman felt terrified that the man would somehow find and approach her. She considered running out of the building but imagined the perpetrator waiting for her outside. She was thinking of calling the police when the librarian finally returned and told her there was no male in the work area where the exposer had been. This was all done in "hushed" tones and dismissed as something that was unfortunate, but over with, as if it was now time to just get back to reading. The woman insisted someone walk her to her car and never returned to what had been her favorite hangout, the county library.

One young man I treated in therapy shared about his school teacher's behavior. Rob, age 13, was close to a male teacher at school. The teacher offered to drive Rob home from school. Before arriving at the student's house, the teacher parked the car and told Rob to watch as he masturbated. Rob sat there stunned and afraid. Rob liked the teacher very much and felt a profound sense of betrayal when his teacher exhibited himself. He felt hurt and lost his trust in a very important adult in his life.

One of my friend's step-father would masturbate in front of her. This lasted several years. She felt responsible for him doing this and was afraid to tell her mother.

I write these stories to help you realize the pervasiveness of abusive behaviors. How could you really know—only recently has it become even nominally common for a victim to speak up, to report abuse, to say "me, too."

If Something Is Fishy...

Children, being easier to control, are often victimized repeatedly before anyone finds out. They have irrational fears of being abandoned or of getting in trouble for the perpetrator's behavior, as they believe what the abuser tells them, i.e., not to tell anyone or they'll be sorry they did. A teacher once told me that she had tremendous regret and guilt for second-guessing herself when she had picked up on signals of abuse (of her sixth-grade male student). When he didn't come to school for several days, she learned that the boy was in the hospital...he had cut his wrists. "Poor Dustin," she said. "I knew there was something fishy going on." Being alert and responsible enough to report your suspicions could save a child from repeated abuse and actually could save his or her life. Here are some red flags that caused a responsible adult to become suspicious, who later found and put a stop to abuse:

- 8-year-old girl lying on couch with her father, watching TV, is walked in on by a house guest who is appalled that the little girl is naked.

- A grandfather takes his five-year-old granddaughter out to the barn every evening after dinner; one day her grandmother sees that the girl refuses to go, and gets the girl to confess what's been going on.

- A woman visiting her sister wonders why her sister wants her to watch as she bathes her 11-year-old son, clearly embarrassed as he stands in the tub.

- One of my friends was kissed on the mouth and touched all through her childhood by a friend of the family. When she told her mother, the mother brushed it off. She did not tell her father because she knew her father would "kill him." She finally told a high school guidance counselor and authorities intervened.

- Several children were fondled at a day care center by one of the staff. Sometimes she rubbed their stomachs, buttocks, or inner thighs while at other times she actually touched their genital or breast areas. The center's director became suspicious when so many of the children seemed afraid of that one staff member.

- Sometimes children will be made to rub the sexual organs of an adult while the adult does the same thing to them. A teen girl was forced to watch her mother's boyfriend masturbate, and was eventually coerced into participating. She tried to avoid him but was often left with him as her "babysitter." She was afraid to tell her mother because she felt her mother would be angry with her. The mother found out when the boyfriend actually joked about it, and had him arrested.

- A babysitter reported to the parents that their 7-year-old son asked her to kiss his penis when she was tucking him into bed. It was later discovered that a male neighbor had taught the child to perform fellatio on him, telling him that all the neighborhood kids did it, and to be in the secret club, he had to, too.

- When "bathroom humor" becomes an obsession or too explicit, find out why the child is thinking about private areas of themselves or others so much. One little boy, Evan, walked in on his mother peeling a cucumber in the kitchen and started laughing hysterically. It was later discovered that an older boy had taken Evan and a friend to his "fort" and sodomized both the boys at the same time, using his penis as well as a cucumber.

- A child psychologist colleague of mine said that she was frustrated and appalled that even after confronting her 8-year-old patient's parents, they saw nothing wrong with having intercourse, nude, in front of the child, who they made sleep in their bed. They told the psychologist it was best that they be in charge of their child's "sex education." Meanwhile, he had developed a nervous tic and did poorly in school. He was eventually referred to therapy by the school's child psychologist.

Unfortunately, many times no report is made. One woman who caught her live-in boyfriend taking photos of her 13-year-old daughter while the girl was asleep (nude) told me, "I didn't want him to be labeled a sex offender. He'd lose his job."

CHAPTER 4

CLUES, SIGNS, AND RED FLAGS

There are many red flags to be aware of, often seemingly small things that may or may not mean anything untoward, but really MUST be checked out if we are to accomplish our mission of putting a stop to and preventing sex abuse. Here are some to note:

SUDDEN VOCABULARY CHANGES: If a child or teenager starts using inappropriate language you need to find out where they heard or learned to use the words. You may hear a child call his or her childhood friend abusive names such as "little prick," "whore," "fag," or other harmful labeling which attacks the child's sense of self-worth, and this may mean the child is repeating what they have themselves been called by an abuser.

In one case, a teacher overheard an 8th-grade female student tell her friend that her mother would not call her by her name, only by the term "slut." Fortunately, when the teacher gave the girl a private opportunity to tell her how things were going at home, the student opened up and said that her mother was extremely jealous of her (she was pretty and well-developed for her age) and was always accusing her of "doing" the mother's boyfriend(s). The girl became visibly upset when she spoke of the boyfriends and the teacher became alarmed. Educators are trained to know it is their responsibility to report suspected abuse, and should follow their own state's procedure through Child Protective Services. They can file the report and trust it will be followed up on, and that the report will be treated with care so that the family will not know who filed it.

Another example of sexual abuse via language was a 15-year-old boy, Danny, who did not measure up to his father's idea for him to be a star athlete and a "lady-killer." He became withdrawn and depressed, and grew even thinner which angered his father. He was not fulfilling his father's fantasies, so when the father drank, he called Danny a "pussy" and a "fag." The more Danny was sexually abused in this way, the more withdrawn he became. Eventually he was referred by a school psychologist to seek therapy.

Children who are being sexually abused are like radios, transmitting signals of their plight, either consciously or unconsciously. They are saying, "Please help me!" although most of us are unable to receive the transmission or choose to disregard the signals.

Youngsters often do not tell anyone of the abuse because of the shame ("I am bad"), guilt ("I must be making this happen to me"), or fear of the perpetrator. Many children won't tell anyone because they are sure no one will believe them and they feel they are responsible for whatever is being done to them.

The following are some of the things that ARE happening. What I want for all of us who care about protecting the innocent is to understand that becoming aware is a critical first step, but bringing light to what's hidden in shadows and learning effective prevention is what is called for right now, right here.

Amy is seven years old. These are some of the ideas in her head: "Mommy and Daddy won't believe me that Uncle Tony told me to take off all my clothes. Who will believe me? He's Daddy's brother. Everyone will think I'm lying and I'll get spanked. Everyone likes Uncle Tony. He buys me and my family lots of presents and comes to our house a lot for dinner. He even dresses up like Santa Claus at Christmas. I used to think Uncle Tony really was Santa Claus. No one will be mad at him, only at me."

According to Beth, age eleven: "Daddy told me not to tell anyone he gets in my bed at night and makes me feel his thing. He tells me that no one will believe me, anyway, and that if I do tell, I'll be sent away from home to live in an orphanage where kids are beaten up. He also says Mommy will get sick if she knows and maybe she'll even die. I love Mommy. I don't want her to die."

All children, whether they are victims or not, feel omnipotent about some things. In child psychology, this means the child thinks he is able to make events happen in his life just by wishing it so or feels responsibility for bad things that happen to others.

Here is what I discovered that Scott, aged eight, had in his mind: *What if everyone finds out that Mr. Brown asked me to let him touch me in private places. He's my coach. Everyone will think that I wanted it to happen to me because I am very bad. If they find out, my friends will think I'm dirty and they'll call me a fag.* I share examples like this with you to emphasize that more abuse is taking place around you than you realize. It is still, tragically, hidden in the shadows and swept under the rug. Don't let that dissuade you from shining a light into the dark corners or looking under the rug. We must.

Abused children sometimes try to give more than a signal and come right out and tell someone of the abuse. Then the fear of not being believed can become a reality. "I told my grandma that Mr. Smith was making me pull up my dress in school when no one was looking. She said I was a dirty little girl who should have her mouth washed out with soap," said Amy, aged ten.

Because small children are not clearly able to explain sexual events due to their limited vocabulary, they may send out signals which need to be investigated further. For instance: "Mommy, I don't want Jimmy to babysit with me anymore." It is important to ask, "Why?" If the child becomes evasive, the parents need to gently but firmly push for the answer. Sometimes children think they have revealed the secret, but no one picks up the signal. A child may say: "Jimmy wears underwear with polka dots." This statement is a definite cause for concern and needs to be pursued. Such a transmission must not be ignored.

Very often a sexually abused child enjoys the abuse (i.e., the attention, physical pleasure, or rewards like coins or candy) to some small degree, which increases guilt many times over. The child becomes fearful that someone will discover that he or she likes being touched in a sexual way. For instance, boys may (automatically) get an erection. When treating victims, it is necessary to get the child to admit that the act was somewhat enjoyable. It is important for the child to hear that all of us enjoy a sexual touch but that we still wish the abuse had not happened because of the pain and guilt involved. Once the child can admit he felt pleasure, but the incident was in no way their fault, the guilt can be alleviated.

John, aged five, was sexually abused by a male through anal penetration. John got an erection during the act and it took several sessions to get him to tell me about it. His feelings of inadequacy came out when he drew a picture of himself at my request. He first drew a head, eyes, mouth, ears, and then suddenly the head was given long hair, make-up and earrings. He handed me the picture obviously confused as to his sexual identity since he felt as if he had been used sexually as a female. He had been fighting in school in a most aggressive manner, which was due to his trying to reestablish himself as a male. Beating up the other little boys and getting power over them was his way of handling feelings of being less than masculine.

Offenders frequently give children bribes to ensure silence. This is particularly confusing for the child if the abuser is a baseball coach or another person in a respected position who the child genuinely admires. These two factors create a conflict, which conspire to overwhelm the child. He feels guilty about taking the bribes while liking them at the same time, especially if he gets something important like a favored position on the team.

Look for unexplained gifts or money possessed by the child. The child may sometimes unconsciously want to reveal these gifts because he wishes the abuse to stop. This is a form of signal telegraphing what is happening and is a definite danger sign.

Such signals are constantly being transmitted but usually are not received. Sometimes parents or people who work with children have a feeling something is wrong somewhere with the child but try to deny it. It is frightening to consciously admit to ourselves that such a horrendous act is happening when we would rather pretend to ourselves that everything is okay. We don't know what to do so we use that old defense—denial.

There are those adults who themselves were sexually abused as children and have worked hard for many years to bury these incidents. The unresolved feelings may be raising havoc in the adult survivor's life, but he chooses not to deal with issues for many of the same reasons a child won't tell (i.e. fear of the censure, shame, guilt, feeling dirty, etc.). These adults do not want to recognize sexual abuse in others because all of the old feelings that have been repressed will come rushing back.

Therefore, it is especially important that any adult who works with or around children be aware of having been sexually abused. Many adults, including some therapists and teachers, blatantly avoid the issue of sexual abuse with clients or students, even if they know the signs. Sometimes this denial is due to their own incestuous wishes or fantasies. Dealing with the sexual abuse, especially incest, could be much too threatening.

All children have incestuous feelings toward their parents at various stages of their lives, as it is a natural phenomenon. However, a lot of adults grow up thinking they are truly perverted for feeling a sexual attraction for a parent because of society's taboos against incestuous desires. The shame causes them to bury the feelings. Recognizing sexual abuse would stir up old, shameful feelings.

Most parents also have sexual feelings toward their children at times. Feelings are different from actions but some adults cannot separate the two concepts and feel guilty about being attracted to a child, again because of societal taboos. These people will also not want to pick up signals from a sexually abused child.

For this and other reasons, it is imperative that abused children be treated by therapists who specialize in treating sexual abuse victims and adult survivors. Trained therapists are aware of the feelings experienced by sexual abuse victims and are conscious of the transmissions these children emit. Abuse victims require very specific therapy geared towards treating the psychological effects of sexual victimization. A trained therapist is more likely to have resolved his own issues around sexual abuse if there has been any in his life. Most importantly, the therapist is able to confront the whole area of sexual issues openly. This openness regarding sexuality is essential as the child is not only treated in therapy, but also educated in avoiding future sexual abuse.

Therapy should not focus on the child's sexual behavior but on feelings such as anger, aggression, depression, loss of power, guilt, and all the other feelings connected with being victimized. The issues for the child are feelings associated with the victimization rather than the sexual aspect of the abuse.

Physical Signs of Sexual Abuse

Physical signs of sexual abuse are much more concrete than emotional ones and leave little doubt that sexual abuse has occurred. Physical signs will exist only if the child has been penetrated vaginally or anally, handled roughly, or in some cases, because of pregnancy. A vaginal discharge, spotting from the vagina or anus, urinary tract infections, or difficulty with sitting or walking can indicate that the child has been sexually abused. Rough handling will, of course, leave bruises or cuts. Pregnancy is sometimes the result of a girl being molested by a male in the household and many times the girl ignores her condition for weeks or even months, preferring to stay in denial, even to herself.

Emily, aged 14, relates: "What am I going to do? The doctor said I'm pregnant. My daddy's the father. Now everyone will know our secret. I am so ashamed! Maybe I'll lie about who the father is. Mom keeps asking me who it is. I won't tell her so she slaps me and calls me a slut. I just want to die."

In school, teachers may notice that the abused child urinates frequently, pulls at his pants, masturbates in class or other inappropriate places or displays his genitals to other children and for teachers. The child may also show an unusually high interest in seeing and touching sexual parts of other children or adults. All of these actions reveal a preoccupation with and worry about the abuse. A first-grader enticed a boy on the playground to slip behind a tree and look up her skirt. The teacher saw them and the boy was punished, not believed when he said it was all the little girl's idea. Later it was discovered that she had been molested several times by her grandfather.

The point that sexually abused youngsters are interested in the genitals needs amplification. These children may have an unusual interest in the sexual parts of people or even animals and may actually fondle the sexual organs of adults, children, or pets.

An agency social worker related: "Our agency had to remove two girls from one of the foster homes we utilize. Another girl, who had since left the home, told the agency that she was sexually abused during her stay there. The family had been taking care of foster children (most often girls) for many years. It soon was learned that when the foster father was an adolescent, he would often exhibit his genitals to both children and adults and would even masturbate in the presence of others. The chances are very good that this foster father himself was a victim of sexual abuse. Residents of the small town where he grew up would dismiss the boy's exhibitionism/masturbation by saying, "Oh, he's just trying to get attention." The fact is that he *was* transmitting a very strong signal which people could not deal with and, therefore, ignored.

Children who have been abused may come to school dressed in several layers of clothing, even on a hot day. They may even refuse to remove the excess layers. The child in this instance is trying to get a feeling of protection from the clothing.

An abused child may be unwilling to change clothes for physical education class because of a fear that others will find out about the abuse, especially if there are bruises or other marks on the breasts or genital area.

Case notes of a colleague: *Mary, age four, will not pull her pants down when her nursery school teacher takes her into a bathroom unless the teacher turns away. Mary has been sexually abused by her mother's boyfriend. She is frightened of revealing her genitals to anyone.*

Although most children are abused by someone they know through seduction, some are sexually molested in a public place. Any such child will then fear returning to the facility where he was molested. A child who fears public bathrooms or showers may have this fear because he has experienced sexual abuse in these areas.

Case notes: *Roberto, age 8, refuses to go into public restrooms when his family goes out to dinner, is travelling, etc. His parents cannot understand why he panics and they become impatient when he insists that his dad accompany him to the bathroom. His parents think he is just being "difficult" and his father tells him to "grow up."*

The sexually abused youngster often refuses to remove his clothing to go to bed. The child feels the clothing is a barrier to prevent access to his body.

Sleep disturbances are almost always present in sexually abused children. The child may have nightmares about being abducted, falling, or acts of violence rather than a replay of the abuse. Our fears most often appear symbolically while we sleep, often in the form of nightmares. The fear of abduction and the fear of violence represent feelings of powerlessness, lack of control and vulnerability. If the child has been abused in bed, he may be especially frightened of falling asleep and may wander around tired the next day.

Appetite may be affected by sexual abuse. The child either may lose it or begin to stuff food in an uncharacteristic way. A loss of appetite may be related to a depressed and hopeless feeling. A common symptom of depression, even in adults, is cessation of appetite. Stuffing may be caused by a desire to fulfill unmet emotional needs. The unmet needs have mostly to do with the need for power, control, and acceptance of oneself, which have been stripped away by becoming a victim. A good therapist will look behind the eating disorder for potential abuse as a root cause.

There may also be psychosomatic complaints—i.e. stress-produced headaches, stomach aches, and other physical disturbances.

A child who has been abused may suddenly begin to exhibit regressive behavior such as bedwetting, thumb sucking, talking like a baby or throwing temper tantrums, going back to an earlier period of his life, which seems to give the child a degree of comfort because he is returning to a time when he felt safer.

A school psychologist recorded: *Gary, aged 5, has been sexually abused by a trusted adult neighbor. Gary has become very difficult to handle at home and in kindergarten. He insists on not following rules that he previously had learned to follow, such as going to bed on time, eating with utensils instead of his hands, and staying in the yard. When his parents try to control him, he throws himself on the floor and screams. He has also begun wetting his bed and can often be found sitting in corners working his thumb.*

Even small infants are sexually abused to the point of contracting venereal diseases, if they are penetrated vaginally or anally. These babies often have a condition called "failure to thrive syndrome," i.e., they do not develop normally, either physically or emotionally. Babies with *failure to thrive* suffer from a lack of nurturing from a parent or mother substitute. The caretaker has little concern about meeting the baby's needs, so no bonding occurs between the mother and the child. For instance, in many cases, the baby's cries will be completely ignored. After a time, the baby learns that crying does no good and so stops. Then a sense of hopelessness sets in and the baby becomes completely apathetic. Physical and mental development do not proceed at a normal rate. Because the child is being ignored by the caretaker, and does not react fearfully to strangers, a perpetrator has much easier access to the baby to sexually abuse him. It is important to remember that in most cases of sexual abuse there are no physical signs, which makes detection more difficult.

The Behavior and Psychology of Sexually Abused Children

Sexually abused children have recognizable behavior patterns which may help detection. Teachers are in the prime position to receive signals of sexual abuse from their students.

DISTANCING: A child who suddenly becomes distant from his teacher might have a sexual abuse problem. Some abused children have a fear of people who are the same sex as the perpetrator who is victimizing them. Some will exhibit indifference toward or active avoidance of all sexual references or potentially sexually-arousing situations.

Case notes: *Tommy (aged 9) has been fondled on his penis by his older cousin. His father does not understand why Tommy will not hug him anymore and why Tommy avoids his male relatives at the big family gatherings which occur every Sunday.*

SEDUCTIVE BEHAVIOR: On the other hand, the child may have an opposite reaction of behaving seductively to adults and children. A youngster is more likely to be seductive towards others rather than avoiding possible sexual situations, if he or she has been victimized over a longer period of time. Long-term abuse conditions the child to believe that it is necessary to be openly sexual to obtain love and affection. The victim displays seductive or sexually provocative behavior inappropriate for his or her age. The child may try to kiss other children or adults on the mouth in a prolonged version of a "French kiss." He may try to sit on people's laps or brush against others in a provocative manner. Attempts to crawl into bed with other children or adults are common.

Case notes: *Janet, age 12, has a father who has just gotten remarried. Janet's stepmother notices that the child often sits on her father's lap and tries to French kiss him while rubbing her hands all over his chest. She likes to turn on the stereo and do seductive dancing for her family.*

A few weeks ago, Janet traumatized a 10-year-old boy, whose parents are friends of the family, by sitting in his lap in a car and fondling him on various parts of his body as well as trying to kiss him. Unfortunately, Janet's father will not talk to his new wife about Janet's actions. It is possible that the father is the abuser or that, even if he isn't, he denies the possibility of abuse because he cannot face it. He may also deny the possibility because of other, less severe emotional problems than those of a perpetrator.

The victim learns from the perpetrator that seductive behavior is the way to obtain affection. A young female victim may walk, talk, and behave in a seductive manner.

Case notes: *Jeanne, aged 14, comes to school wearing heavy make up with her hair in what she considers a sexy hair style. Long, dangling earrings hang from her earlobes. Her feet are adorned with very high heels and she is usually wearing a tight skirt and low-cut blouse. She swivels when she walks and openly flirts with male teachers.*

Abuse victims can often be observed coming on to classmates or teachers and other adults. Affection and sex have gotten all mixed up in the child's mind and he eventually learns to use sex as a way to get love and acceptance. Victims often grow up to be exploited and victimized sexually and emotionally as adults. There are many in-depth books and resources for these victims in need of healing, including 12-Step programs based on the principles of Alcoholics Anonymous, such as SLAA (Sex and Love Addicts Anonymous) https://slaafws.org/ Remember, each and every victim of sex abuse needs to be identified and given tools, resources and professional help for healing, no matter how recent or distant the abuse occurred. One way this helps our mission is that a healed victim is much less likely to become a perpetrator themselves, an unfortunately common occurrence. I don't know what percentage, but I do know many SLAA members are sex abuse victims. Here is what the web site posts to help people determine if SLAA could be a fitting group to assist in healing and leading a healthier life:

Characteristics of Sex and Love Addiction ©The Augustine Fellowship, S.L.A.A., Fellowship-Wide Services, Inc. All Rights Reserved

1. Having few healthy boundaries, we become sexually involved with and/or emotionally attached to people without knowing them.

2. Fearing abandonment and loneliness, we stay in and return to painful, destructive relationships, concealing our dependency needs from ourselves and others, growing more isolated and alienated from friends and loved ones, ourselves, and God.

3. Fearing emotional and/or sexual deprivation, we compulsively pursue and involve ourselves in one relationship after another, sometimes having more than one sexual or emotional liaison at a time.

4. We confuse love with neediness, physical and sexual attraction, pity and/or the need to rescue or be rescued.

5. We feel empty and incomplete when we are alone. Even though we fear intimacy and commitment, we continually search for relationships and sexual contacts.

6. We sexualize stress, guilt, loneliness, anger, shame, fear and envy. We use sex or emotional dependence as substitutes for nurturing care, and support. 7. We use sex and emotional involvement to manipulate and control others. 8. We become immobilized or seriously distracted by romantic or sexual obsessions or fantasies.

9. We avoid responsibility for ourselves by attaching ourselves to people who are emotionally unavailable.

10. We stay enslaved to emotional dependency, romantic intrigue, or compulsive sexual activities.

11. To avoid feeling vulnerable, we may retreat from all intimate involvement, mistaking sexual and emotional anorexia for recovery.

12. We assign magical qualities to others. We idealize and pursue them, then blame them for not fulfilling our fantasies and expectations.

SEXUAL ACTIVITY: Sexual abuse can be discovered when a child is caught engaging in sexual activity with another child. The abused youngster initiates the sex play in an attempt to overcome his own feelings of being powerless and helpless. If he initiates sex with someone else, he is in control and won't feel so much like a victim, at least temporarily.

Case notes: *Brian and Sam, both seven years of age, were discovered by Sam's mother engaging in sexual behavior together. The discovery led to the uncovering of several months of sexual abuse of both boys, by an 18-year-old neighbor who both boys looked up to as a big brother role model. Both youngsters felt an intense betrayal of trust. Sam and Brian, through their duplication of the abuse, were trying to regain a sense of control and power. There were repercussions when the other children in school found out about the abuse. It was a very painful and humiliating experience when other boys in the school taunted them with such comments as: "Where are you going, little faggot boy?" or "Don't let that fag play with us."*

In therapy, both boys spoke of how angry they were with the perpetrator for causing them to be ridiculed and how painful it was to have teasing compound the pain of the abuse. Neither boy wanted to go to school at all, but had to go eventually and submit to the pain. Neither boy would walk to school alone and both had nightmares because they feared the perpetrator would literally kill them since they had "told." The therapist conducted further research and discovered that the perpetrator had told them he would kill them if they told anyone about the abuse.

INABILITY TO CONCENTRATE: School performance often takes a plunge after an abuse incident and there is pulling away from other youngsters and adults, including teachers. A child may show an inability to concentrate because of worry about the abuse. He can be preoccupied with thoughts of the next incident or can simply be burned out emotionally. This is another opportunity for teachers to pick up danger signals. Donnie, aged ten, focused on doodling and drawing instead of listening to the teacher's lesson. Rather than simply reprimand the boy, the teacher kept the boy after class to discuss the drawings, which were not clear. That is when the boy shared his anxiety about what his mother made him do with her ever since his father had passed away.

LONER BEHAVIOR: The child may be a loner because of his worry that someone will find out about his terrible secret. In incest cases, the child probably has always been a loner as the family has kept the child out of activities and somewhat isolated him from friends.

Sexually abused children often feel isolated because their own peers are too naïve. The child has experienced adult behavior and feels distanced from peers who act their ages sexually.

Case notes: *Mary, aged 14, lives the very painful life of an incest victim. Mary's father has sexual intercourse with her on a regular basis. Her father won't let her go to school dances or ball games or invite friends to come home with her. He doesn't want her to make friends because she may then reveal the abuse to them. She is afraid of making friends because she, too, wants to keep her terrible secret because of her shame and guilt. She feels isolated and alone.*

ABSENCE FROM SCHOOL: A sign that teachers should look at is frequent absences of a girl whose father writes the excuse notes. The father is home during the day and convinces her to stay with him. This kind of situation is often related to parentification (i.e. taking the place of a parent).

PARENTIFICATION: Girls in incestuous families take the place of a mother in areas of caring for the father (cooking for him, doing his laundry, etc.). She will also take care of her brothers and sisters, clean the house and do everything else that a mother usually does. Because of having to perform these duties, she experiences a feeling of not knowing exactly who she is in terms of her role in the family. She is the child on one hand, and is the "woman of the household" on the other. This conflict and stress of performing as an adult can cause her to feel depressed, suicidal or make her feel like running away, as victims often do when they become older. She may also experience a false maturity which causes her to appear sophisticated and grown up. Underneath, she is just a frightened little girl terribly in need of nurture and someone who has her best interests in heart.

Case notes: *Gina, aged 15, often stays home from school to be with her father, who works the night shift. Her mother works during the day so Gina takes care of the house and her father, both in and out of bed. She is tired of doing all the housework and being expected to be grown up and do grown-up things. She feels angry because she cannot do what other girls her age do – i.e., go to parties, go out with boys, and just generally experiment with life. She doesn't feel like she's developing and wakes up most every morning feeling depressed, used, and under enormous stress.*

SEXUALLY DRAWING AND PLAYING: Sexually abused youngsters produce bizarre art work of a sexual nature, such as drawing people with gigantic penises. Their play with other children, or their stories, are sexual at times. A victim playing house with another child often recreates the abuse. Therapists will use dolls with younger victims to help them act out the traumatic events. Children seem helped and relieved after they have told the whole story. Then they are able to get the feelings of hurt, anger, and humiliation out.

COMPLIANT BEHAVIOR: Overly compliant behavior is a sign that the child feels powerless and out of control. The children have been conditioned to be victims and have difficulty asserting themselves. Children, as well as adults can be conditioned over time through fear and domination to be almost completely submissive, to the point they seem very, very lost.

Because a victimized child feels vulnerable, powerless, and unprotected, he will often withdraw from other children and adults, because he has transferred the betrayal of trust caused by the offender onto others in general. Children who have maintained a trust by non-abusers may cling to others to provide what they feel is a protective shield around them. Clinging feels safe and, therefore, becomes exaggerated. There is a fear of being alone because the protective shield is gone, and the child feels very vulnerable and unable to protect himself.

Case notes: *Judy, age 13, is pushed around and bullied by the other children in school and in the neighborhood. They push ahead of her in the cafeteria line, throw her books in the mud and pull her hair and she just generally places herself into a victim's role. She clings to her homeroom teacher who is a female and seems to have a fear of her male teachers. Judy's brother and his friend have been sexually abusing her for the last two years. On several occasions they have ganged up on her and have raped her.*

LACK OF TRUST: A lack of trust can be present as the child's faith has been shaken. His trust in others is seriously damaged in the present and this can affect all future relationships. There has been no protection of his body or personal space.

Case notes: *Sandy, aged 11, has been sexually abused by her mother, who makes her sleep with her. Sandy's mother will not let her have any friends. She was very happy recently when Mary, from her class, asked her to sleep over at her house. Sandy asked her mother if she could go to her new friend's home and her mother became quite angry and said "No." Sandy feels suffocated by her mother who people call "crazy." In actuality, Sandy's mother is so emotionally disturbed that she considers her daughter a part of herself emotionally. To lose Sandy's close presence would mean to lose herself. Someone with Sandy's experience might not trust teachers or other adults.*

In this extreme case of mother/daughter incest, the mother, because of her deep emotional disturbance, confuses herself with Sandy, both emotionally and physically. The mother lacks a reality based personality.

DAMAGED GOODS SYNDROME: One of the most prevalent signs in sexually abused children and adult survivors is a "damaged goods syndrome." The child feels worthless and damaged beyond all repair. Low self-esteem, depression, and even suicide can be reactions to the feeling of being damaged goods. Extremes of behavior and dress are typical of a child who feels like damaged goods. He may be boastful and exhibit attention-getting behavior to compensate for the low self-image. On the other hand, he may appear downtrodden and apathetic. The manner of dress may also fall on either end of an extreme pattern. One child may dress flamboyantly, while another is always unkempt and sloppily dressed, making a statement that he or she does not care.

POSSIBLE SERIOUS MENTAL ILLNESS: Some authorities believe childhood psychoses and even the development of multiple personalities are in part or wholly due to early childhood sexual abuse. It is theorized that children develop these illnesses as a defense mechanism against painful sexual trauma.

The following is a summary of the signs of sexual abuse in children. Each sexually abused child reacts differently to being victimized. All children exhibit a different combination of signs. Not all of the signs pertain exclusively to sexually abused children. For instance, nebulous signs such as a lack of trust or low self-esteem can come from other causes. However, other signs such as venereal disease, damage to the genitals and other physical signs are strong indicators of sexual abuse. Detecting sexual abuse is a matter of knowing all the signs and then carefully assessing the child's behavior and feelings. It is rather like putting the pieces of a puzzle together.

SIGNS OF SEXUAL ABUSE IN CHILDREN

Physical

Girls -vaginal discharge, spotting

- Boys or girls–signs of penetration

Hiding Clothes

- To conceal that they are torn or soiled

Tugging at Pants

- Preoccupation with sexual abuse

Excessively Bulky Clothing

- Makes child feel less vulnerable

Clothes to Bed at Night

- For protection

Changes in Appetite

- Eating loss because of depression or eating more because of stress.

Sleep Disturbances

- Usually present in sexual abuse. Child has nightmares about being kidnapped, falling, or violence rather than a repeat of the sexual abuse. If the child is abused in bed, the child may be frightened of falling asleep and may be tired the next day. Fear of sleeping alone, fear of the dark, fear of going to bed.

Failure to Thrive

- Baby does not develop physically and mentally at a normal rate. Often ignored by caretaker. More vulnerable to sexual abuse.

Difficulty with Walking or Sitting

- Physical trauma to genitals.

Bruises in Genital Area

- Child has been handled roughly.

Urinary Tract Infections

- Especially in girls, due to swelling and bacteria from genital stimulation.

Venereal Disease

- Genital to genital contact has occurred.

Pregnancy

- Significant if girl refuses to tell who the father is or she denies pregnancy.

Unwilling to Change for Physical Education

- Afraid to reveal body in fear the others will find out about abuse.

Bedwetting, Thumb-sucking

- Regressive behavior—child goes back to earlier, safe period of his or her life.

Fear of Showers or Bathrooms

- Frequent sites of sexual abuse.

Psychosomatic Complaints

- Develops stomach aches, headaches, as a response to stress.

Behavioral

Fear of Being at Home

- Often comes to school early and leaves late.

Extreme Fear of Being Alone with Men or Boys

- May fear males if abused by a male.

Masturbation and/or Displaying Genitals

- Preoccupied with abuse.

Sex Play with Peers or Toys

- May start sexual activity with another child to overcome victimization and become controller.

Aggression

- Especially obvious in boys who have been abused by another male. To fight other boys equals establishing masculinity.

"Loner" Behavior

- Child doesn't want anyone to know about abuse. In incest cases, family keeps child out of activities—also children feel peers own age are too naïve.

Inability to Concentrate

- Especially in school—child is worrying about abuse—preoccupied with next incident, escaping situation or are burnt out.

School Performance Difficulties

- Especially if sudden.

Truancy

- One danger sign is when only one parent writes excuse notes. This parent is alone with the child all day.

Unexplained Gifts or Money

- May be bribes taken from perpetrator.

Pseudomature Behavior

- Victim appears grown up and sophisticated. Girls of incest families have taken mother's place (caring for parent, house, siblings, etc.).

Sexual Knowledge Beyond Age

- Children who can describe cunnilingus, fellatio, rectal or vaginal intercourse have learned firsthand (observation or participation).

Clinging Behavior

- Great need for reassurance.

Overly Compliant Behavior

- Child feels powerless and out of control—is a victim and cannot assert self.

Anger

- Especially if child has told someone and that person doesn't help. Becomes angry at everyone.

Bizarre Art Work, Plays or Stories

- Especially if sexual.

Seductive Behavior

- Learned from perpetrator as a way to get affection. No other male role model available. Will be seductive toward teachers, classmates, and other adults.

Running Away

- Child trying to escape.

Withdrawal, Depression, Suicidal Feelings

- Reactions to feelings of hopelessness.

Psychological

Lack of Trust

- Child's trust has been abused—affects trust in future—"no one to protect me." Terrified of relationships—no protection of space or body.

Powerlessness

- Child feels like a victim and feels vulnerable.

Affection and Sex Mix-Up

- Used as power currency
- Using body—child getting what he wants.

"Damaged Goods Syndrome"

- Victim feels worthless, damaged forever.

Guilt

- Feelings of having done something wrong.

Low Self-Esteem

- Feels worthless, used.

Blurred Role Boundaries and Role Confusion

- In incest (involving father or step-father) situations, child takes mother's responsibilities—confusion about whether she is wife or mother.

Fear of Abuser's Threats

- Perpetrator often tells child no one will believe if he tells. Child also told she will be sent away or Mother will get sick. Abuser may threaten bodily harm.

Fear of Being Alone

- Frightened of further abuse.

Serious Mental Illness

- Possibility of childhood psychoses. May develop multiple personalities as a defense mechanism.

CHAPTER 5

SEXUAL ABUSE, EDUCATION AND PREVENTION

Like prisoners in a cell, both children and adults in our society have been "protected" from the knowledge of widespread sexual abuse by the invisible walls of societal taboos. Remember, for every case that is revealed, there are many more which remain concealed. Until that fact is understood and incorporated into society's awareness, preventing and stopping abuse will not be comprehensive enough.

When abuse occurs, victims and those who want to help them must venture out from behind the walls, past the taboos. This leaves both victims and the people who might help them in a state of culture shock, often denying the reality of what has happened.

What purpose does denial serve? Doesn't it make more sense to hear and act on the truth in order to protect ourselves or others? One remarkable woman, Svali, escaped the abuse of living in a cult in the 1990's and has written, at great risk to her life, many articles about abuse, mind control and denial. From svalispeaks.wordpress.com, we can read about denial, information from a very compelling perspective:

"You know you're making all of this up, it isn't true. I certainly don't remember any of the things you are telling me." The speaker was my mother, two years ago, and she was telling me in no uncertain terms that she did not believe me. Her amnesia is intact and strong, protecting her. I had confronted her about the fact that she and I had spent a lifetime in the cult, and that I loved her and wanted her to get out. I had told her specific names of people we both knew in this phone call, the first time I had spoken with her in a year. "Mom, you're dissociative, that's why

you don't remember," I told her. "No I'm not, nothing happened," she maintained.

... I have never, ever told my son that he is making it up when he deals with memories. I pray with him, and ask God to heal the memories, and to bring security to my son, and to fill the painful areas with the knowledge of His love and mercy. I pray for blessing on both of my children. And God has been faithful to answer. My son no longer nightmares at night, has made good friends at school, is active in sports, has better grades than two years ago, and tells me he is happy (the last is the most important to me).

I believe that denial is a large barrier to healing. Often, when a survivor begins to recover memories, they will go to family members for validation, or to confront them. They are also frequently faced with invalidation, denial, or even verbal abuse from those same family members, who need to maintain their own denial to protect themselves from facing painful truths. "You're crazy," "You're sick," "You have a sick imagination," "How can you make these things up?" "You need help," and more cruel phrases are thrown at the person whose amnesia is beginning to break, from those who want them to maintain it.

After all, if ONE person starts remembering, then OTHERS might, and the others in the family system might not be psychologically strong or healthy enough to remember. I think one of the saddest realities is that it takes more psychological integrity, honesty, and truth-seeking to remember something as painful as childhood abuse, yet the person who is remembering is told the opposite by family members unwilling to face their own pain.

The disapproval of family members is extremely painful, and is enough to cause some to doubt the reality of their own memories. "Maybe I am making this up, otherwise why don't THEY remember?" the survivor thinks. Or, "I love my parents/siblings/cousins and I don't want to hurt them. What if they're right?"

When memories are first recovered, they often come in flashes that last a second or two, are vague, and may seem unreal to the person remembering. Add the message from others that is loud and clear—it is NOT okay to remember—and the survivor may shut down.

Denial may also come from within. It is a basic protective mechanism when a person is confronted with pain; how often do we CONSCIOUSLY deny our own faults ("It wasn't my fault, I was having a bad day, and everyone was against me") to protect our self image ... The more painful the blow to the self concept (since people desperately want to maintain an image of themselves as "okay"), the greater the need to deny.

If events that a person went through destroyed their ability to accept themselves as a worthwhile human being (and sexual abuse does this to the maximum), then they will need to deny that it occurred in order to function in daily life. This is one reason why once the denial is let go of, functionality may temporarily falter in the survivor, as they process the horrendous truths of a childhood filled with pain. It is also a reason why denial can serve a protective function, and should be let go of slowly, carefully, with the help and support of a competent therapist.

Society's taboo cloaked in denial allows abuse to continue and victims to remain untreated, often to become perpetrators. Educating the adult public and, through them, our children, can break down the walls and break the cycle of the sexual abuse taboo.

WHY CHILDREN NEED
SEXUAL ABUSE EDUCATION

To Prevent the Effects of Victimization

A sexual abuse experience overwhelms a child, robbing and depriving him in many ways of his trust in other human beings and his feeling of worthiness. The experience can be relived in a new context in therapy, restoring the child's personal pride and trust. Without the restoring force of the therapist's caring and treatment, the child's mind can only "repress" or attempt to forget the experience.

A child often builds walls to cope with the overwhelming experience of sexual abuse. The walls are built to block experience and feelings from his conscious awareness.

The walls consist of denial—"it didn't happen to me"—or repression— "I forgot it happened to me." The coping or defense mechanisms of denial and repression keep the child from experiencing the feelings associated with being victimized. However, the walls which are erected are not strong enough to prevent leaks, like those that drip through a dike. The feelings are still there and not dealing with them seriously affects the child's personality. He may "act out" his feelings, which is a way of getting them out nonverbally. Common ways of revealing the leak or "acting-out" are stealing, drug or alcohol addiction, promiscuity, suicide attempts or other self-destructive behavior.

Societal taboos, repression, denial and attempts by the perpetrator to ensure silence can all join forces to keep the child from telling about the abuse—most victims do not even tell their parents. The result can be deeper and deeper repression followed by more serious acting-out behavior, making it more and more difficult to restore the child's mind to a healthy state. Many victims go on to become adult survivors, their lives continually showing the debilitating effects of the abuse.

"The most determining factor in shaping my personality, relationships, and entire life was most certainly the sexual abuse by my grandfather when I was ages 5-10," therapy patient Bobbi shared. She lacked any "real" relationships, she said, until she was over 40 years of age. Not into drugs or alcohol, it remained a mystery for years why she could never seem to get her life together. She married and divorced three times, and struggled with her career even though she obtained a college degree. Only after the birth of her two daughters did she start to "wake up," she said. In a therapist's office, she confronted her parents who had known of the abuse but done nothing to stop it. Only after that did she begin to heal and become a person capable of honest and intimate relationships and a functional life.

The aphorism "an ounce of prevention is worth more than a pound of cure" is particularly true regarding abuse. Educating children about sexual abuse can help them break down the taboos to help them resist abusive advances. Even if they cannot resist the abuse, the education can help them to reveal what has happened to those who can help. Educating the adults around them to know the signs of abuse and giving the strength to face it can enable those adults to provide an atmosphere in which the child can tell them of the problem or at least give the adults the courage to put the child into therapy.

Case notes: *Davy, age 7, was left in the care of his older cousin, Bill, age 25, on several different occasions while his parents attended social functions. Davy was sexually abused over a period of time by Bill who gave Davy money not to tell about the abuse.*

If Davy, in the case above, had been educated about sexual abuse and how people who are close can abuse, he might have been able to say "no." The abuse continued for several months, ultimately causing severe emotional damage.

Too many times I have seen cases where the parents assumed the child would tell them about unwanted touching and behaviors of others. Especially if the child has not been taught, repeatedly, what he or she should do, say, and tell their parents, it cannot be assumed the child will prevent or report abuse. It's just not in their psychological make-up, with rare exceptions.

To Compensate For the Limited Availability of Treatment

Unfortunately, there are many areas of the country where treatment for abused children is not available. In these locations education is even more crucial. In many communities, there is a sore lack of programs to serve sexually abused children and a dearth of psychotherapists trained specifically to treat sexually abused victims. Because of the psychological walls of the sexual abuse taboo, many of the people in power in communities would rather deny that abuse exists; therefore, they do not support creation of treatment programs. Even in communities where treatment exists, many psychotherapists may be uncomfortable with treating sexual abuse victims because of their own fears.

Because of the Difficulty of Treating Perpetrators

A majority of perpetrators cannot be brought to the point where there is any degree of assurance that they will stop victimizing children. Many will not admit they are sexual abusers, or do not want to give up their sexual activities with children and therefore do not recognize any benefit in treatment. Some perpetrators are untreatable because they actually are sociopathic; this means that they have absolutely no guilt or sense of wrong-doing about using children sexually. Psychological treatment depends heavily on the existence of remorse in an individual's personality. Without it, treatment is virtually impossible.

Because Sexual abuse is Frequently Not Disclosed

There are many perpetrators who are never apprehended, as children often do not report sexual abuse because of a lack of education on the subject. As a result, even the treatable ones are slipping away to continue to victimize. Parents often assume incorrectly that their child will tell them about being sexually abused. No parent can safely make this assumption. In a study of 411 sexual offenders, researchers Abel, Mittelman, and Becker discovered that the average sex offender who begins to victimize in adolescence may be expected to abuse 380 victims during a lifetime. The perpetrator is allowed to spread his misery to such a large extent mostly because children do not "tell." The longer a victimizer operates, the more his behavior becomes ingrained and addictive.

Because the Perpetrator's Power is Subtle and Seductive

Perpetrators entice children into sexual situations through their position of authority as adults or by communicating incorrect moral standards to children. Many children are lured into abusive situations when perpetrators tell them, "Everyone does it," and "If you tell, no one will believe you." The child feels he has no right to refuse an adult and submits sometimes because the sexual approach is so unexpected that confusion sets in and leaves him vulnerable. Children are taught to obey adults and are socialized to respect the power of adults. Sexual abuse generally consists not of an isolated incident but of a gradual seduction that may take weeks or even months.

Types of subtle force applied to ensure the child's silence about the abuse include making such statements as: "I'll give you money if you don't tell," "I'll hurt you if you tell," "I won't love you any more if you tell," or "Mom won't like it if you tell." The perpetrator often is allowed to have the power to abuse because he seduces the child slowly. The child gradually becomes accustomed to increased intimacy which enables him to overcome his fear and to adjust to the situation. The abuse is often progressive and becomes more serious over a period of time unless a child is educated and able to interrupt the seduction. A frequent pattern is a tickling game, which leads to fondling which may progress to either oral sex or vaginal or rectal intercourse. The perpetrator's power over the child increases slowly unless the child is fully aware that an adult is not allowed to take control of his body.

Because Perpetrators are Frequently
"Wolves in Sheep's Clothing"

Sexual abusers are not easily identifiable. This makes it easier for them to get past a child's and the community's detection. They are not perverts who jump out of bushes naked, nor are they violent, aggressive, or senile. They are not, typically, the "dirty old man" many of us imagine. In fact, perpetrators are generally young or middle-aged. They usually do not exhibit crazed or bizarre behavior nor are they sadistic. They are as likely to come dressed in a three-piece suit or a coach's uniform as to be adorned in jeans or work clothes. Perpetrators lurk in all social classes in all schools, and in all communities. They can be wealthy, poor, bright or dull; they can live in a high priced neighborhood or in a shack.

Because Even Friends Can Be Wolves

Most children who are sexually abused are abused by someone they know well. Recent studies reveal that only 10-15% of abuse is performed by those we identify as "strangers." Mere warnings about strangers leave children unprepared for what really can happen and unprotected from the real danger. Children are usually abused not only by someone they know well but by someone they also trust, such as a neighbor, friend of the family, teacher, or relative. Most abuse follows a pattern of seduction, progressing from gradually more intimate behavior without much physical contact to marginally inappropriate behavior, to touching the child sexually but pretending the touch is accidental. The abuse can end this way or progress further. Even if it ends this way the child has a sense of discomfort and needs to know he needs help and that such behavior is "not okay."

Many of us were taught as children not to talk to strangers. We really didn't know why, except that there was an implication that strangers would kidnap us or in some way hurt us. There was no mention specifically that we could be sexually abused. Actually, abuse occurs at a far greater frequency than kidnapping. The omission was probably due to our parents' extreme discomfort, something many of us share, about discussing sexual abuse with our children.

Case notes: *Jane, who is now grown up, related that her mother told her not to talk to strangers, implying some nebulous danger. While walking downtown one day, Jane saw a man that she had never seen before coming toward her and her mother. Jane asked her mother if the man was a "stranger." Her mother giggled nervously, causing the child to be confused. It was years later that Jane came to understand that the question illustrated her incomplete sexual education. Her mother's nervous laughter indicated her discomfort and fear of the sexual abuse taboo. Many people have this reaction as a defense mechanism when certain subjects are discussed that touch off feelings they would rather avoid.*

Because We Often Misunderstand the Definition of Sexual Abuse

Sexual abuse often consists of less than full vaginal or anal penetration. Most times the child's genitals are handled or he is asked to handle the perpetrator's genitals. Sometimes there may be oral sex. There may be attempts at penetration, but rarely does it occur, except with the fingers. Physical contact may not even occur. There are instances when a child is made to undress in front of the perpetrator or the abuser exposes himself to the child. My personal experience with adult survivors indicates that even incidents in which there was no physical contact with the child can be traumatic. It can be traumatic for the child even with no physical contact. It can leave the child with a sense of being exploited and used with consequent feelings of mistrust and shame. Children can learn through education that sexual abuse is not necessarily confined to being touched.

Case notes: *Mary's father used to stare at her breasts when she was an adolescent. Mary felt very uncomfortable and had many of the subsequent negative feelings of a sexually abused child who would have been touched. She felt ashamed and guilty and walked stooped at the shoulders to hide her "shameful breasts." It was not until she entered therapy that she was able to talk about the feeling of degradation produced by stares. She felt like "damaged goods." Mary needed someone to tell her it was normal to feel degraded and that those stares had been sexually abusive. Mary was relieved to find that her negative feelings about the abuse were valid. She now walks straight and doesn't stoop over at the shoulders.*

WHO SHOULD EDUCATE CHILDREN

Every community in the United States has a school system. The system generally works well, and has vast resources. Why not use it to teach children about sexual abuse? The answer seems to be that local school officials fear the wrath of parents who would come back to them embittered because Johnny has been taught that Aunt Martha can't kiss or hug him.

Or, just as sex education in schools remains controversial, there is no clear agreement about what non-academic teachings the school should be involved in, versus leaving many important topics (like prevention of abuse) up to parents. As a result of these attitudes, the most progress many districts have accomplished is the presentation of a "Good Touch, Bad Touch" program which, in effect, teaches children not to let anyone touch them anymore if it is uncomfortable.

This kind of program is helpful, yet fails to warn the child that literally anyone he comes in contact with can abuse him—even a trusted teacher or relative. He does not know about the seductive nature of abuse, which enables the abuser to approach the child and to lure him in without the child realizing how demoralizing and harmful the experience is. He does not know that a trusted, even beloved, person can use an experience that at first may actually feel good, to ultimately make him extremely uncomfortable.

District officials must learn that parents who object to sexual abuse education in the schools are not reacting to the realities of abuse or our children's needs. They react to the time honored taboos which have protected adult abusers and non-abusers alike from facing those realities. Who needs protection more, the children or the adults? It's time the school districts began to consider taking responsibility for teaching all children of school age about sexual abuse.

For the youngest victims, parents are the only people who have access to these children for educational purposes, so they must teach pre-school children about abuse. Parents who have educated their children in sexual abuse have opened up the lines of communication. If the child is sexually approached in the future, he will feel more comfortable in telling the parents after being educated. Through education, the parent has a chance to refute the perpetrator's claim that "everyone does it" and that the child has no right to say "no" to an adult. Most important of all, the parent can assure the child that he will be believed if he tells someone.

THE WALLS THAT BLOCK
SEXUAL ABUSE EDUCATION

Adults have had many years to erect large and imposing walls to block action toward sexual abuse education. There are many reasons for these walls. One is fear of emotional damage to the child. Many people are afraid to discuss sexual abuse because they are fearful of making the child distrustful of any affectionate behavior from an adult. They do not want to see a youngster become "paranoid." The fear is partly rational, but may be more related to taboos rather than rational fears. The fact remains that effective abuse education will not make a child fearful of affection and sex.

We teach our children not to cross a street in front of a car yet we neglect their safety in the area of sexual abuse. We need to understand that teaching children to avoid abuse is a kind of safety issue. Statistics reveal that children have a greater chance of being sexually abused than hit by a car. We tell them repeatedly about the danger of crossing the street but don't worry about making them paranoid about cars. Cars are okay to ride in and for people to drive, but there are important rules to learn in order to stay safe. So it needs to be with sexual abuse education. A child can learn to discriminate between affection and abuse, just as they can differentiate between riding in a car and being struck by one.

There are emotional walls possessed by potential educators which block discussions about sexual abuse. It is simply not a subject most of us like to discuss with anyone. Parents always find it especially difficult to discuss sexual abuse with their children. It is even more difficult if parents or teachers were sexually abused themselves as children. The hurtful feelings engendered by the abuse may come to the surface if they try to discuss the subject. These persons need to resolve these feelings if they are to educate their children in this difficult issue or even recognize the symptoms if their children have been assaulted. This is why, as previously mentioned, parents tell their children about "strangers" while ignoring abuse that may come from friends, neighbors, relatives, and even members of their own families. The image of a sexually abusive stranger is more comfortable for them.

Parents may also tell their children to avoid kidnapping which is more comfortable than discussing abuse, because it doesn't involve sex. Actually, sexual abuse occurs much more frequently than kidnapping.

Often parents are blocked from discussing sexual matters in general which makes it almost impossible for them to discuss sexual abuse. They must overcome their fear of sexuality before they can approach the subject. Parents naturally want to avoid creating a mental picture of their child being abused because of their fear of the child's pain, so they rationalize by saying to themselves, "Sexual abuse isn't a real danger . . . it hardly ever happens," or, "It only happens to other people's children." Of course, these parents are so strongly blocked against dealing with abuse that they refuse to face reality. Ironically, they leave the child open to the act which they fear so tremendously.

Sometimes children are not educated about sexual abuse because parents do not know how pervasive abuse is. Some people still think that living in a "nice" neighborhood protects their children from abusers. All children are vulnerable to sexual assault. Victims have low, middle level, or high I.Q.s, and can be of any race, religion, or social class.

Some people do not educate children who have not yet reached adolescence because they believe abuse only occurs to puberty-age youngsters. However, children between the ages of 8-13 are those most likely to be abused, and there are many confirmed cases where even infants have been abused.

Another misconception which interferes with abuse education is the belief that only girls are sexually abused. This naivety, lack of awareness, or state of denial is counterproductive to keeping children safe. One mother said to me, "My son was never around Catholic priests or homosexual men, so I never imagined he could be a victim of sexual abuse." Actually, boys get victimized frequently. Recent studies show that although one out of five girls will be sexually abused before the age of 18, the same fate awaits one out of 10 boys. Parents can become strong enough to overcome the sexual abuse taboo through education. It is vital that all adults refuse to allow their fears to interfere with the education and protection of our children.

CHILDREN HAVE BLOCKS, TOO

Children themselves can be blocked when it comes to being educated in sexual matters, including abuse. If education is not started early enough, he may be too embarrassed at the sudden introduction of the topic to handle it emotionally. This occurs because he, too, has become socialized to believe the sexual abuse taboo. Sexual abuse education, like more generalized sex education, can and ideally should begin at an early age, even two or three years of age.

Children who have been educated and, therefore, who are not emotionally blocked, know how to deflect sexual approaches and can defend themselves.

Just learning to say "no" can be an effective deterrent. Even if the child does not report abuse the first time it happens, education may help him to approach an adult to discuss it before it becomes more involved and longer-lasting.

METHODS OF PROTECTING CHILDREN AGAINST SEXUAL ABUSE

There are two basic ways we can provide a child with protection against sexual abuse. Both methods must be used if we wish to decrease the child's vulnerability to the devastating effects of victimization.

The first method has to do with the way a child is raised and how people in his world treat him. This kind of protection is called emotional strength. It can be given to a child in various ways by parents, teachers, and other adults. No matter what kind of abuse is visited upon a child (penetration, oral/genital contact, mutual masturbation, exhibitionism, etc.), he feels helpless, betrayed, and inadequate. He senses an imbalance of power. In the case of incest, the feeling of powerlessness is even more acute because the child depends on the perpetrator for survival (both emotional and physical).

It is essential that children be prepared emotionally to avoid sexual abuse. This is a vital part of the education process.

The second method constrains specific education on sexual abuse itself, including help for parents, teachers, and other adults in educational techniques, which will be effective. Assistance will also be provided to help an adult handle a situation where the child reveals the abuse.

Before proceeding to the specifics, we should understand just what the effects are of such protection. Although sexual abuse can occur even if a child has a good self-image, the chances are significantly reduced. Further, the training has the effect of making it easier to restore self-esteem in therapy. This is because the child who has been trained in abuse knows that the abuse was not his fault—that the responsibility lies entirely with the offender. An abused child who does not understand this may ultimately become a victimization-prone individual who can repeatedly be taken advantage of by the perpetrator who, of course, inevitably preys on children who are full of self-doubt.

We can give our children the building materials to construct strong barriers to protect them from not only sexual abuse but other types of victimization through building self-esteem by praise and non-critical correction. Circumvention of victimization also includes teaching children not to accept sexual stereotypes, developing closeness with the child, teaching the child not to obey adults blindly and communications to him that he has the right not to have affection forced upon him by even non-offending adults.

Now that we are familiar with the basics involved, we can move on to discuss the specific areas dealt with by complete abuse education.

Giving a Child Self-Esteem

The most important protection against sexual abuse that a child can possess is a good self image. The child's ability to say "no" to sexual abuse often hinges on the child's feeling of worthiness and a security that can only be born of a strong ego. Some children get victimized time after time while others never do. Frequently, in incestuous families, if there are two or more children, some will become victims, some will not. Very often the child's inner strength is the deciding factor.

Every child experiences life very differently from every other so that each child's personality is uniquely developed. Parents react to and raise each child in a family in different ways. In addition, each child grows up in his own individual environment. The combination of all his experiences, which are unique to only him, determine his ability to effectively live his life. A consequence of his experience can result in great ego strength which will help him deflect sexual abuse or poor ego strength which may leave him more vulnerable and open to victimization.

If parents help a child feel special and cared about, then the child will not be so willing to be used to feel important. How does a parent go about the difficult task of helping children develop self-esteem? It is really quite simple in theory but hard to do in practice because parents are imperfect human beings whose emotions are not always under control.

The next two subjects are examples of effective techniques for giving the child self-esteem. One good way is to give children praise that is specific and accurate. For instance, "You are such a good girl" will not have the impact of such statements as these:

"I like this drawing because the colors are so bright and it shows you worked hard on it."

Or:

"Grandmother seemed to like the flowers you picked for her and I think she appreciated your consideration."

It is important that praise be based in reality. Children have a way of sensing when praise is real and when it is manipulative or artificial, just as adults do. Another way is to understand that children often make mistakes which anger parents. It is important when a parent talks to the child about a misdeed that the parents stick to the issue and not attack the child's worth. An example of constructive criticism: "I don't like the way you walked through the house in your muddy shoes. Please take them off at the door next time."

An example of destructive criticism:

"You are such a slob. Everywhere you go you leave a mess. You tracked mud all over my carpet. Don't you have any sense?"

Read both statements while putting yourself in the child's place. It is easy to realize which statement leaves a child's self-worth intact.

Reprogramming Sexual Stereotypes

Boys and girls both are vulnerable to sexual abuse, but for different reasons. Girls are taught in our society to please other people, especially adults. They are taught by word or actions that they will feel good about themselves if they please others. Thus, they may try to please an offender by succumbing to his requests. Boys, on the other hand, are taught to be big and brave. Needing help is considered somewhat weak. Because of a boy's desire to handle problems themselves, they may not tell anyone that they are being sexually abused. The feeling has to do with fear of being a "wimp." We must teach girls that men do not exist on this earth to take care of them. If we don't, girls will be open to the so-called "protectiveness" of the offender.

The most effective method of combating sexual stereotype expectations for both boys and girls is role-modeling. For instance, if a child observes his father showing vulnerability by expressing his feelings, crying sometimes, and accepting support for problems, the child is more likely to learn that he doesn't have to be "macho" to be a man.

Unfortunately, the double standard is still alive and well. It implies that men can be aggressive in obtaining sex any time, any place. Society sanctions the right of males to use women sexually. A possible consequence is that a potential sexual offender may be encouraged to pursue females of any age for sexual purposes. Children need to observe people participating in sex with a sense of responsibility in an on-going relationship and not just for self-gratification. Both married and single parents are able to role model a caring intimate relationship. Fathers and mothers who use others sexually are harming their child's chances of gaining a sense of respect for sexual activities. Mothers who use sex as a bargaining tool to obtain what they want from their husbands or fathers, who seem to want their wives mainly for sex or other servitude, are setting a poor example of caring and consideration within a relationship.

Developing Closeness to Children

Sometimes youngsters feel alienated from their parents because their parents do not communicate with them or seem very interested in them as people. These children are especially susceptible to offenders who offer "friendship," "love" or "special sharing" which is missing from their relationship with their parents and which they need very much. Regular communication with a child and expression of interest in his life is essential. Then, even if abuse does occur, it is less likely to continue over a long period of time as the child feels close enough to disclose the secret. Tanika and Andy are two children who are being sexually abused:

Case notes: *Tanika, age 10, is invited into her male neighbor's house at least twice a week when his wife is at work. The neighbor, Al, invites Tanika in for milk and cookies. She likes to visit Al because he listens to her worries about schools, stories about her friends, and her sad feelings about her parents, who pay no attention to her. Al makes Tanika feel both important and likeable. Recently, Al has begun to ask Tanika to lie down on the sofa with him. At first, he kissed her a lot on the mouth and has now progressed to taking his penis out of his pants and rubbing it against her body. She is very uncomfortable and wants Al to stop lying down with her, but she doesn't know how to stop him. She is worried about losing the only relationship she has with a sense of belonging. Tanika does not bother to tell her parents, as she feels they wouldn't care even if they knew.*

Andy, age 11, on the other hand, has a babysitter, Andrea, age 18, who, for the first time last weekend, took her clothes off in front of Andy and asked him to watch her masturbate. He felt very embarrassed. She told him not to tell because they had a "special secret," and because "I won't be able to be your friend anymore if you tell your parents." Andy's relationship with his parents is close and he told them the next morning. Andy's parents then reported Andrea's actions to her parents and the authorities. Andy never had to be subjected to Andrea's abuse again.

Teaching Children Not to Respect Adults Blindly

We teach our children every day to respect and obey adults—all adults. Adults are portrayed as important and all-knowing.

Case notes: *Kenny bursts into the kitchen and enthusiastically tells his mother how great his day was in nursery school. Right in the middle of his telling her about specific events, his Aunt Martha walks into the kitchen. The mother abruptly stops Kenny's conversation by saying, "Go outside, Kenny. Aunt Martha and I have something to discuss." Kenny interprets her comment to mean that his conversation is not important and that adults take precedence.*

Because Kenny has learned that adults are more important, he may be subject to a perpetrator using adult supremacy to get him to obey sexually. If children are treated as young adults and not as second-class citizens, they are more likely to feel strong enough to refuse an adult's sexual advance. Another way adults encourage children to obey blindly is illustrated in the following example:

Case notes: *Carol says to her mother that she doesn't like her mother's new friend. Her mother may say "That's ridiculous," or "How dare you say that?" or, "What does a kid like you know?" This same parent would probably not make these statements to a friend. Why take away a child's power to have his own feelings about an adult?*

Other ways that Carol's mother could have responded to Carol's comments are: "Why don't you like him?" or "Let's talk about it." One of these approaches would have helped Carol feel more like a respected individual whose feelings are important.

Children need firm boundaries around their own private territory even in a family. We should always respect a child's privacy in his bedroom and in the bathroom. No adult should invade a child's territory by entering it without permission. If a child is not respected in this way, a perpetrator will have an easier time invading the child's space as the child has come to accept invasion. Because children are taught to respect and obey adults, they feel that adults are more likely to believe another adult than a child. This is the reason it is so easy for offenders to manipulate their victims into cooperation by telling them, "If you tell, no one will believe you." Adults, in the child's eyes, have greater credibility.

If the adults in a child's life respond to the child's fears (such as fears of the dark, of dogs, etc.) by saying, "Don't be ridiculous," or "Stop acting like a baby," the child does, indeed, learn that people will not believe him. If he is abused, the perpetrator can convince him that he won't be believed if he tells.

Never Allowing Affection to be Forced on Children

How often are babies passed from person to person at a big family gathering? The child is being treated like a human football and cries every time a stranger holds him. We sometimes allow our babies to be tweaked, patted, and even fondled in public. If we do not intervene, the child learns that he must permit adults to touch him, even when he doesn't like it. After all, he is expected to "obey." Youngsters need to learn that if they don't like someone's touch, they can and should say "no." A child should be taught that the only criteria he needs for saying "no" is that he is uncomfortable with what is going on. A baby obviously cannot say "no" and needs adults to protect him and to teach him that his body is not public property. For instance, Tish's mother told a group of relatives the following shortly after Tish's birth:

"I know this family likes to pass the babies around. It's fun to make them laugh by the tickling and tossing up into the air. Soon Tish will be old enough to pass around. However, I will not feel comfortable if you do that with Tish. If you want to talk to her or make her laugh, please leave her in the playpen or high chair."

Last week when Tish was sitting in the grocery cart, an older man came up to Tish and was tickling her to make her laugh. Tish's mother asked him to stop, which he did. Children often have little control over who touches them, how, or when. The child's rights are ignored. According to Pam, now an adult:

Case notes: *When I was a little girl, my Uncle Harry would tickle me unmercifully and my parents would let him do it. Uncle Harry loved to hold me up in the air. I was screaming with fear and was struggling. My parents watched and didn't tell him to stop. I felt powerless and unprotected. I felt I was expected to allow Uncle Harry to handle my body since my parents didn't intervene.*

Because of a child's dependency on adults for protection and their feelings that adults are all powerful, the child may assume his parents realize that an offender is abusing him and that it is okay to turn over control of his body.

Case notes: *Katie, age 10, is held on her grandfather's lap at a family reunion. Katie feels awkward, especially when he moves her on top on something that feels like a large, hard bump to Katie and she is confused and frightened. No one notices what is happening to her. Because Katie thinks her parents are all powerful, she believes they know what is going on (they in fact, do not know) and that they, therefore, approve of what the grandfather is doing.*

Children are taught that adults are always right. So when a child is being sexually abused, he is often confused because it is uncomfortable and awkward, yet because the person doing it is an adult, he assumes it must be all right. Adult can tell children when they are wrong but youngsters are not allowed to tell adults that. Children learn, by implication, that adults can do anything they want at any time even if it includes a person's body.

Giving a Child Technical Knowledge
—When to Educate—

Most of the time, sexual abuse education is given to a child after the abuse occurs. It's like locking the barn door after the horse has gone! Walls of protection are of very little help to a small person who has already been victimized.

Educators must consider sexual abuse education to be basic safety information. Many adults want to wait for the child to ask about sexual abuse. Most children are unlikely to ask because they do not even know what it is or that it even exists. We cannot afford to wait until they ask, if ever, because of the seriousness of the consequences.

Sexual abuse education needs to proceed at the same pace as sex education in general, i.e. slowly and geared to the child's age, becoming more detail oriented as the child grows in age and maturity.

We must teach the child sexual vocabulary because the child can develop a sense of shame about his body when parents have a hard time talking about sexual parts. Their fears can convince him that the subject is taboo. An example of this is the use of frivolous terms which may convince the child that his parents do not wish to deal with the subject. If he figures the subject is taboo, he may then be less likely to report being sexually abused because it seems not to be a subject to be discussed.

Further, it is very difficult for a child to report sexual abuse without a good working vocabulary. Frivolous names for body parts make it very difficult for children to communicate effectively about sexual events.

Teaching the Child Vocabulary

The first step is to give even the smallest child a vocabulary for body parts. We have no difficulty teaching a child the names of his knees, eyes, or nose, but most parents get embarrassed about teaching a child such words as "penis," "breasts," and other sexual identifiers. An ideal time to teach a child about sexual areas is when they are having a bath. It seems more natural for the parent and the child to do this when the child is already undressed for another purpose. Also, an abuser may try and redefine words such as "tickle." Children must be taught enough vocabulary to be able to describe activities to their parents accurately. For example, "Uncle Dan likes to tickle me" may not mean what the parent first assumes; it could mean that the child is being molested.

For parents or teachers or other adults who are having trouble saying sexual terms, it often helps to stand in front of a mirror and practice saying words aloud to help overcome embarrassment, or meet with other parents who are also committed to education and prevention.

Handling a Child's Natural Fear of Sexual Abuse

Making a child paranoid is not the goal of sexual abuse education. For that reason, in discussions about sexual abuse with very young children, combine the subject with other safety issues (looking before crossing a street, not petting strange dogs, etc.) so the child is not unnecessarily frightened of abuse. If the subject is presented in too potent a form, he may become fearful that every teenager or adult he comes in contact with may abuse him.

There can be so much fear that the child may withdraw from others or have bad dreams about perpetrators. Fright can also cause the child to be traumatized to the point where he will not wish to discuss sexual abuse at all in the future. The training can backfire by making the topic of sexual abuse a taboo subject for discussion for him. The consequence of this is that he may be blocked to further education about the topic or may not report his being sexually abused to anyone if abuse happens to him.

It is awkward to sit a child down across a table and, in a formal manner, launch into the subject of sexual abuse education. There are many opportunities to discuss sexual abuse naturally so that the atmosphere can be more relaxed than if the parent takes the initiative formally. Depending on the child's age, television shows regarding abuse could be excellent triggers for conversation and so are newspaper stories. Recently a cartoon was published that addressed the sexual abuse topic through using the well-known comic hero, Spider-Man. It was "produced in cooperation with the National Committee for the Prevention of Child Abuse." The purpose of the cartoon was to educate children about how to protect themselves from abuse as well as to teach them what to do if they are abused. It illustrated that abusers can be familiar and trusted people who either touch or ask to be touched, or both. Furthermore, it was illustrated that a child is not powerless and has the right to say, "no." Blogger Jared Mace (blogintomystery.com) comments:

...good for Marvel for letting Spider-Man, their flagship, their biggest icon, be a victim of the abuse upon which the comic is trying to shine a light. Nothing could better drive home that this could happen to anyone, and that having it happen to you doesn't make you a bad person, quite like a real genuine superhero going through the same thing. There was probably a suit somewhere that cautioned against this choice, arguing that doing something like this would damage the almighty brand. Maybe not. But the fact is, Spider-Man is presented here as a victim of sexual abuse in his youth, and he made it through. That's a powerful message to the people with single-digit ages that make up the target audience, and a good one.

Sometimes a child may say something pertaining to sexual abuse that the parent can use to introduce the topic. One of the best places to talk to a child about abuse is in a car. The parent's attention is not fully focused on the child who then feels more relaxed about discussing a topic such as sexual abuse. For example, cars are a great place to discuss what hitchhikers sometimes do to people. This conversation could become a springboard to talk of forced sexual abuse vs. seduction. The initiation of the subject can occur naturally rather than in a contrived way. Having it happen informally helps the child and parents both to be more relaxed and less anxious with this emotion-filled topic.

The more the subject of sexual abuse is discussed, the more specific the discussions can become. Discussing the subject will also generally become less painful for both the child and the parent as taboos are gradually broken down.

How We Teach the Child to Know
When He is Being Abused

It is effective to explain to the child that grown-ups and even some other children may ask him to do something he does not want to do. You can say it this way: "Someone may try to touch a place your bathing suit covers." The child needs to know that he should say "no" and tell his parents or another adult. He needs to understand that keeping secrets about such activity will cause him much pain, and that telling about it will relieve that pain and give little pain to others. Most children can understand the idea of someone older using his power to bully and take possessions away. Such a situation should be correlated with a bigger person using power to do sexual things. A parent can say, "Someone wanting to touch you in an uncomfortable way is kind of like if someone was breaking or taking your toys. It is not okay and I want you to tell me."

You should be aware that a child may be confused about what sexual abuse is even after it has been explained and described. He will learn much from examples of real-life sexually abusive situations. For instance:

"Someone may…

    put their hands down your pants

    ask you to lie down with him

    rub against you

undress in front of you,

show you his penis

want to take pictures of you with no clothes on

kiss you on the mouth."

The child must learn that he does not have to get undressed for anyone, including even a doctor, unless he knows why. Before a child is taken to a doctor for a full physical examination which requires removal of his clothing, he should be told that the doctor will examine parts of his body which are usually covered up. Smaller children, especially, need to be taught that a doctor's office is one of the very few places to get completely undressed in front of someone outside the immediate family. However, it is important that you accompany your child into the doctor's office as, in a few circumstances, doctors have been known to be sexually abusive. Following is a current example:

Headline news, January 2018 (cnn.com):

Once a world-renowned sports physician treating America's foremost Olympic women gymnasts, Larry Nassar now will spend the rest of his life behind bars.

The disgraced former USA Gymnastics and Michigan State University doctor was sentenced to 40 to 175 years in prison, a judge announced Wednesday, after more than 150 women and girls said in court that he sexually abused them over the past two decades.

Assistant attorney general Angela Povilaitis:

"The breadth and ripple of this defendant's destruction is nearly infinite.

No coach should be in a shower with a boy. No priest has an excuse for any type of sexual touching. But Nassar perfected a built-in excuse and defense — he was a doctor and a good one, or so the world thought...

What does it say about our society that victims of sexual abuse have to hide their pain for years when they did nothing wrong? What does it say about our society when victims do come forward and they are automatically met with skepticism and doubt, treated as liars until proven true? What do we take away from this? These have been important narratives to hear and witness and listen to. They will be the words that burn down cultural stereotypes and cultural myths. (Add If these victims had received sexual abuse education, they may have known that Nassar's actions were wrong. They also may have known, through education, that doctors and other professionals may also be perpetrators. If the parents were aware of sexual abuse signs, they, too, might have minimized Nassar's long list of victims. Education is prevention!)

Judge Rosemarie Aquilina: "Your decision to assault was precise, calculated, manipulative, devious, despicable. I don't have to add words because your survivors have said all of that. ...You can't give them back their innocence.

You do not deserve to walk outside of a prison ever again. You have done nothing to control those urges. And anywhere you walk, destruction will occur to those most vulnerable.

I've just signed your death warrant."

Identifying Abusers

Children as young as two years need to know at least a bare minimum about people who are potential abusers, i.e. that abuse is usually carried out by familiar people, not strangers and that perpetrators use the subtle force of bribery ("I'll love you if you let me touch you," "You can come and see the puppies if you touch me," "This is our special secret," etc.) and seduction (progressively more intimate sexual activity). Most children, if uneducated, think sexual abusers are crazy, violent people. This belief leaves them wide open to the advances from those most likely to abuse them, i.e. "friends" or family. A child needs to know that "nice" people can bribe him or try to convince him to do something he does not want to do so that he cannot be taken by surprise.

The risk of abuse is further reduced if children realize that perpetrators are usually middle-aged or younger and a few are even teenagers. Most perpetrators are men, some are women. Adults can become very uncomfortable visualizing their child being sexually abused by a baseball coach, grandpa or any other family member, a teacher or other "respectable" people. For this reason, they tend to shy away from giving concrete examples of potential abusers to a child.

But it is necessary to list potential abusers by their positions in the child's life if he is to be sufficiently aware of the potential for abuse. Good and bad touches should be explained. A good touch is a touch that feels good. Ask the child to give examples of good touches. Two might be hugging a dog and holding their father's hand. Then ask for examples of bad touches. That is a touch which feels bad such as another child pulling his hair or sexual touching. A good preventative measure is playing a "What Would You Do If . . .?" game to help the child practice saying, "No." For instance, "What would you do if a man tried to touch your penis?" or "What would you do if someone you didn't know tried to get you into their car?" The child needs to learn that it is okay to feel a touch which was a bad one and that, even if the perpetrator claims it was an "accident," his feelings matter more than those of the perpetrator. He must learn that in these kinds of situations, he needs to obey his own feelings and say "no" and go tell his parents or another adult.

The youngster needs to know that his father or mother will protect him if the parent is there and that the parent will not allow strangers to pick him up or otherwise touch him. Furthermore, a parent needs to communicate that he will allow no one to kiss the child if the child does not like to be kissed by particular persons, even if they are relatives.

Warning a Child About Babysitters

Babysitters are an area of concern which needs to be addressed with a child specifically. Children should be told to obey the babysitter in specific areas only (meals, bedtime, etc.) and should be told in what areas not to obey. They are not to obey requests they do not understand and should not allow themselves to be bribed or threatened into doing anything which feels uncomfortable. The sitter should be told the child can say "no" if he does not understand a request. If a child suddenly dislikes or fears a babysitter, the parent needs to investigate why.

Case notes: *Robin, age 8, used to look forward to times when Chuck, a neighbor, would be babysitting with her. Chuck is an 18-year-old college student who babysits nights and weekends to earn money for college. Robin has suddenly become very withdrawn when she finds out he is coming to stay with her. When questioned, Robin admitted that Chuck had been touching her legs and vagina.*

This is an example of the fact that those in authority are not always right and that includes parents, teachers, and other adults. We must teach our children this as a basic element of abuse education.

Ten Facts All Parents Should Tell Their Children About Abuse

1. Most perpetrators (85-90%) are well-known to the child.

2. Most perpetrators are men; some are women.

3. Perpetrators are all ages, including older children and teen-agers.

4. Sexual abuse most often occurs in either the victim's or perpetrator's home.

5. Victims are usually young—the average is about eight years of age.

6. "Tell me or someone else if you are abused or if someone tries to. You may not want to always share with me (your parent) throughout your life, so it is okay to tell someone else if that is easier for you."

7. "It is not fair if someone asks you to keep a secret about something you want to tell. Perpetrators may ask you to keep the secret because they know what the consequences will be if you tell."

8. "Your body belongs to you and only you can decide who touches it. Never allow anyone to touch you in places where a bathing suit covers."

9. "Sexual abuse is never your fault."

10. "I will believe you if you tell me you have been sexually abused and will try to comfort you."

Preparing Adults to Receive a Disclosure

Very often, children reveal abuse while being educated either at home or in school. They suddenly realize it is not "right" when given the moral perspective inherent in all good abuse training. Therefore, teachers, parents, and other adults must know how to handle the disclosure before they begin to teach children about that abuse. People who are shocked and outraged only succeed in further victimizing the child. It is extremely important to minimize emotional damage to the child and to speak very calmly at the disclosure.

1. "I believe you." (Most children fear not being believed if they reveal abuse.)

2. "It is not your fault." (Sexual abuse is *never* a child's fault.)

3. "I'm glad you told me—You are very brave." (A child is usually terrified an adult will flip out due to the disclosure.)

4. "I'm sorry it happened."

5. "You may want to talk about it for a long time and may even feel better if you go into therapy to talk about your feelings."

6. "I'll do my best to support and comfort you."

7. "I'll do whatever I can to protect you." (Never promise a child unconditionally that you will protect him from further hurt or that "everything is going to be all right" because the child will have pain and suffering in the future and may keep it in to live up to your expectations.)

8. "I need to tell someone else—it's the law, other people will have to talk with you."

(Detectives, social workers, and attorneys may need to question the child.)

Helping Parents to Accept Their Feelings About Disclosure

If the abuse is disclosed to a parent, the parent's feeling of guilt or anger needs to be put aside to help the child, at least initially. However, it will be extremely important for the parent to work through his anger and guilt. Parents often feel responsible for the child being sexually abused as there is guilt about not protecting the child more effectively.

Parents can strongly share the same feelings as the victim when they discover their child has been abused. A feeling of powerlessness is common. They cannot punish the abuser or change the fact that the abuse has occurred, but they will wish to. Anger is a common reaction and since it cannot be expressed effectively toward the abuser in most cases, some parents become angry, much against their will, at the abused child as if it was his fault he was abused. This causes the child to feel even more helpless. Thus, the victim is blamed and revictimized. In therapy, there often is an emphasis on treatment of the child victim with little attention being focused on the parents who are blaming themselves and possibly their child. It is essential that the whole family be treated as the abuse affects every interrelationship in both directions. Parents can be treated effectively to learn to resolve their guilt and feelings of vulnerability and powerlessness, thereby enabling them to help and support the child and avoid burdening him with their anger and guilt.

Case notes: Michael's father relates:

It's my job as a father to take care of Michael. I let him play with Don next door and even go to the woods. Don built a fort. Don abused Michael there in the woods. Don seemed like sort of a big brother to Michael and my son looked up to him. I never thought Don would do this to Michael. I still feel so guilty and angry every time I think of Don putting his penis in my son's rectum. I want to kill Don. I feel so powerless.

Helping Parents to Talk to the Child After Disclosure

Parents need to encourage the child to talk about the assault; if not now, then later. The child should not be pressured to talk about it.

A way of approaching the child is:

"I love you and want to hear your feelings about the abuse."

"I understand you when you tell me that it's hard to talk about it."

"You seem very hurt and sad. Are you?"

If the child does not want to talk, the conversation can continue:

"It's all right that you don't want to talk about it now. I just want you to know I'm available whenever you want to get mad, cry or just talk. You are very important to me."

Group Sexual Abuse Education

Sexual abuse education can be very effective if conducted in a group setting of 8-10 children. The goal of such groups is not only to impart technical knowledge, but to encourage group discussion of the topic so that children become more comfortable talking about abuse. Talking about abuse in a group setting helps reduce the fear connected with the topic. Unfortunately, it is often difficult to assemble groups of children outside of school. But school district officials are afraid of parents' objections regarding giving sexual abuse education, making it difficult to assemble groups in school, as well. This limits the potential for abuse education in many communities. Religious groups, boy scout or girl scout groups, and other children's activity groups are potential territory for sexual abuse education. However, there is a fear of parental objection with these groups as there is in the schools.

You may have to campaign hard for abuse education to overcome these fears. A psychotherapist who is trained in sexual abuse is the best leader for such groups. You may have to search for such a therapist, as they are in short supply. Your efforts will be rewarded with the best possible training. These groups can strengthen training in abuse given at home. Material for discussion includes:

Define:

1. "Crime," "rape," "sexual abuse," "exposure," "incest," "victim," and "offender."

2. Discuss how each of these concepts is different from one another and how they are similar.

3. Discuss what those being educated would do in certain situations. Play the "what would you do?" game ("If someone asks you to look at him undress," "If someone touches your bottom," "If someone follows you home, what would you do?")

4. Explore how to report sexual abuse (when, how, and to whom).

5. Give technical information such as that which is given under the three previous headings.

6. Encourage group members to express their feelings frequently. Children can have a whole range of reactions from feeling sad that abuse hurts to glad they are learning something that will help them. They need to discuss their feelings on the spot to reduce the fear and intensity of the feelings engendered by this emotional topic. Abuse is sometimes revealed in these groups and the therapist must be prepared to handle the child's disclosure as well as the group's reaction. If one child discloses abuse, the other children will require especially sensitive handling. The group leader should follow the guidelines given above under "Preparing Parents to Receive a Disclosure."

SELECTING A CHILD CARE CENTER

Many parents experience a feeling of loss when it becomes necessary to place their child in a day-care center. For many, working is not an option but necessity, and they regret not being able to raise their children full time.

Reports of sexual abuse at these centers have been publicized nationally. There have even been reports from children placed in many of these centers that they have been pornographically photographed while under care. In some cases, these children say they were transported to other locations where they were sexually exploited by being forced to pose either by themselves or with other children (often the opposite sex) for lewd and suggestive pictures. The discovery that a child has been abused sexually will make an already difficult situation ultra-traumatic. A single parent's guilt, especially over putting the child into day care, will be multiplied many times over.

Case notes: *Heidi, age 32, was recently abandoned by her husband who left her and two small children, ages two and three. Heidi had to find a job and place her children in a nearby center because of the financial circumstances of her separation. Three days after she began receiving care there, her three year old daughter reported to Heidi that one of the staff had rubbed her vagina. Heidi must now lend emotional support to a child who has been horribly hurt at the same time she is making the very difficult adjustment to separation. The pressure of dealing with the reporting authorities will make this already difficult situation even tougher.*

Most day care centers are safe for children, but it would be wise for parents to do the following before entrusting the care of their child:

Find out which agency licenses the program and speak with the staff at that agency about the facility in question. Talk with referral agencies and other community child care agencies to find out whether or not the program has a good reputation.

Ask the childcare center to provide information on the teachers and other staff and talk personally with them. A parent would allow his personal instincts to answer the question, "Do I trust these people"?

Ask the director of the center what the criteria are for hiring staff (in terms of education, police checks, background checks, references, prior employment history, or other important criteria they may use).

Talk with other parents whose children are in or have been in the program. Find out how they feel about it.

Be certain parents are welcome to drop in unannounced at any time during the day and that they can participate in the program if they wish. If parents are forbidden at certain times, this may be a sign that the center personnel have something to hide.

A parent should insist on signing individual permission slips for every field trip. He should not allow the child to be taken away from the center without written permission and specific knowledge of his whereabouts every day.

Be sure the center employees know exactly who may pick the child up from the center and will not release the child to anyone else.

Parents who suspect sexual abuse should do the following:

1. Report your concerns to the local county child welfare agency before confronting the center staff. Do not confront the staff because trying to deal directly with the problem will leave the other children unprotected (see point 3, below).

2. Look for the emotional signs of sexual abuse as described in the previous chapter. Some parents feel they would like to have their child examined for evidence of abuse before reporting it. They need to keep in mind that most sexual abuse leaves no physical evidence.

3. Talk with other parents whose children are also in the center to ascertain whether or not their children are behaving suspiciously. This must be done because some perpetrators deliberately work in day-care centers or volunteer to work in organizations where there is easy access to children. If the parents merely pull their child out of the center when suspicion arises, any perpetrators working there will continue to abuse the other children. It is important for the parents to report the circumstances to the child welfare agency, which will then close the center down for the thorough investigation.

In recent years, day care centers have been required to become licensed. The regulations of becoming licensed are different from state to state, so it is important for everyone to look into your individual states regulations.

For instance, in the state of Florida, the child care licensing program is a component of the services provided by Department of Children and Families. The purpose of the program is to ensure a healthy and safe environment for the children in child care settings and to improve the quality of their care through regulation and consultation. The department ensures that licensing requirements are met through on-going inspections of child care facilities, thus preventing the continuing operation of substandard child care programs. Some religious facilities are exempt from licensure and are monitored through the church with which they are associated.

Even though day care facilities are more closely monitored in recent years, it is still wise to investigate your day care choice as suggested. Licensure does not insure that the system works perfectly giving you a false sense of security.

Bottom Line: Get educated. Pay attention. Trust your inklings. Help others. Like me, become a Sexual Abuse Prevention Advocate.

CHAPTER 6

ADULT SURVIVORS OF SEXUAL ABUSE

Living with the devastating aftereffects of abuse experience as a child has become a way of life for many adults, both men and women. The effects of victimization can seriously impair an individual's capacity to lead a happy, functional, and fulfilling life.

Some have a "victim" mindset, while others have a "survivor" attitude. There is a vast difference in quality of life, depending on the steps taken to healing, and the mindset of the individual. It is important for abused women and men to consider themselves survivors rather than victims. To be a survivor is to have the ability to be strong and to function independently and without a difficult past intruding on and shaping one's everyday life. Victims, on the other hand, consider themselves helpless and at the mercy of others.

Many adult survivors of childhood victimization have never resolved their feelings about being abused and, further, based on my experience, an incredible number have never discussed the abuse with anyone. Many people revealed to me for the first time their sexual abuse experiences when they heard I was writing a book on the subject. They poured out their stories to me, saying they had been too ashamed to reveal their experiences to anyone before.

One woman, age 54, told me: *One summer when I was eight years old, my uncle took my younger sister and me out to the woods several times. He would completely undress my sister and would then lick her on the vagina and kiss her. Then he would take his penis out...and would ejaculate on her stomach after rubbing up against her. He made me watch each time he did it to my sister. My sister and I never told anyone because we were so frightened and ashamed.*

While being horrified at what he was doing to my sister, I remember wondering why he wasn't doing it to me. The thought occurred to me each time that I was not as appealing as my sister. I know the sexually humiliating experience with our uncle has caused both of us a lot of trouble. My sister is an alcoholic and has had difficulty in her two marriages which both ended in divorce. I have difficulty trusting men and getting close to others of both sexes. When you write your book, I want to give it to my sister. We have never talked about what happened, but I think it's time...

A large number of survivors have repressed their sexual abuse experiences because it would be devastatingly painful to remember them. The memories are imperfectly hidden in the unconscious mind where they negatively affect the survivors' everyday lives. Quite often the only way they can be lifted out of the unconscious is through psychotherapy. Some people find hypnotherapy helpful, in conjunction with psychotherapy.

Clients who have repressed victimization may come to a psychotherapist for any number of different reasons and, in the course of therapy, discover that sexual abuse is at the root of their problems. The sudden flood of memories coming into one's consciousness can be overwhelming, scary, and painful—being in a safe environment with a qualified professional is very important.

REASONS FOR DIFFERENT EFFECTS OF SEXUAL ABUSE ON INDIVIDUAL VICTIMS

The degree of emotional disturbance caused by sexual abuse differs from person to person. We are all unique individuals who respond differently to stressful and traumatic events in our lives. In war, some soldiers are emotionally devastated and psychologically wounded while others are discharged with fewer scars and less emotional trauma. The effects of sexual abuse, however, are determined not only by our interpretation and unique personalities but also by several variables of the abuse itself.

These factors include the victim's age, when the abuse was revealed, and the degree of closeness in the relationship between the victim and the perpetrator. Also of consequence is the amount of touching or violence connected with the abuse and the length of time during which the abuse was carried out. Long-term effects also vary depending on the degree of affection exhibited by the perpetrator, whether or not the abuser is a member of the opposite sex, and the prior sexual experience of the victim.

It is very difficult to fully assess the long-lasting effects of sexual abuse on any one individual as emotional damage is by its very nature immeasurable. However, it can be said that each victim is traumatized to some degree. Even though great emotional damage is not inevitable, there is a high risk of permanent devastation.

How Keeping the Secret Worsens the Effects

Unfortunately, most sexual abuse is not revealed until the abused child becomes an adult. By then, the abuse may have caused a major personality disorder and the survivor's day-to-day life may have been seriously impaired. Keeping sexual abuse incidents a secret can greatly increase the individual's anxiety, depression, and/or guilt. The survivor does not resolve the results of the abuse, but rather denies to himself that it ever happened.

A woman I discussed this book with told me that she had always had memories of when and how she was touched inappropriately as a child by her grandfather, yet somehow had never "connected the dots" that this had been "incest" or that she had been "sexually abused." One day she was talking with a therapist about her challenges as a parent of two daughters, and the experiences from her own childhood came to light. The therapist pointed out the obvious—that the woman was an incest survivor. This was shocking "news" to the woman, yet provided a critical puzzle piece to understanding her own adult relationships, issues, and anxiety around being inadequate as a mother.

Very often, abuse is revealed when the person enters therapy as an adult for other problems such as alcohol or drug dependence, relationship difficulties, depression, or other symptoms which are keeping the survivor from enjoying life. The longer the abuse is kept a secret, the more traumatic the effects on the victim. If the survivor feels guilty about the abuse and vulnerable because of it, he is vulnerable to re-victimization, not only sexually, but emotionally and physically as well.

A revelation, even if handled poorly by those whose reactions have an impact upon the victim's emotional state, can be beneficial since victims can handle reality better than trying to "forget" disturbing events.

"Forgotten" incidents or those which are repressed have an insidious way of affecting an individual's behavior and emotions in ways which he is often unaware. Keeping the secret from themselves prevents survivors from resolving the issues surrounding the abuse. Becoming aware of the abuse brings these issues to the surface. They can then be resolved, permitting emotional healing.

How Response to a Disclosure May Change Long-term Effects

If the abuse is revealed when the survivor is still a child, the long-term effects can be partially determined by the reactions of important people in the child's world. If parents, along with teachers and the legal system, are supportive and understanding, the child has a good chance of being significantly less traumatized. However, parents may become angry and blame the child for what happened because they are unable to deal with the abuse. The legal system may subject the child to rough questioning by detectives or an upsetting court hearing. Under these types of circumstances, the child is more likely to feel blame and guilt and develop emotional scars. But if the child grows up feeling more like a survivor than a victim, he or she has a good chance of moving past the incident(s) and developing healthier connections with others.

In some cases, children must reveal or talk about the details of abuse in a police station or a courtroom. Fortunately, many legal jurisdictions are sensitive and caring about their needs. A few jurisdictions still are insensitive. When criminal charges are filed against a perpetrator, the legal system sometimes considers the needs of the victim to be secondary to the prosecution of the case. Survivors, as children, are sometimes questioned in detail in an insensitive manner. They are asked to relate sexually embarrassing activities to strangers during interrogation. Children giving evidence in court in sexual abuse cases need to be given more support because many suffer from stress before a trial.

Sometimes cases collapse because not enough is being done to help vulnerable child witnesses. They have to publicly relieve the most traumatic, upsetting and humiliating experience of their lives in order to try and get justice. A victim of child sex abuse is usually the sole witness to the crime and the strength of the case lies in testimony. It is vital that children are supported by not only a parent, grandparent, or other trusted adult, but also by an experienced child advocate. The child advocate needs to be trained in child sexual abuse cases from either a local service provider or other crime victim assistance organizations. The advocate's support during the trial can provide support both to the child as well as his/her family support person. The advocate has the necessary knowledge as well as resources to make the court process less intimidating.

The court process can also be difficult with testimony in some states being required at both the preliminary hearing and the actual trial. During the legal process, a child can be questioned by police as well as by the prosecuting attorney and cross-examined by the defense attorney. The manner in which the whole legal process is handled is very crucial in determining the long term effects of the aftermath of the abuse. I highly recommend that if you are the parent or guardian who will be supporting your child through the court process, that you go to NCTSN.org (the National Child Traumatic Stress Network)which is a website that can help you and your child cope with the emotional stress of the legal system in its article, "Emotional Impact of the Legal System." Areas covered are "Understanding the role of the legal system in sexual abuse cases, common concerns about taking legal action, fears and realities of going to court, coping with the court process step by step, coping with the verdict and moving on." There are also additional resources listed.

Victims are less likely to be emotionally affected by abuse if they reveal it soon after it occurs. The sooner the abuse is dealt with, the less likely the individual is to feel the effects of keeping the secret (guilt, blame, shame). The revelation is beneficial but, in addition, the more fortunate victims receive great support and help with overcoming the trauma by family members and/or mental health professionals. The victims are reassured that the abuse is not their fault.

When an adult is victimized, they are less likely to blame themselves, deny the abuse, or keep it a total secret. These survivors often have the maturity and good sense to seek out professional help. They may find that sharing their experience with someone with whom they are in a significant relationship can build emotional safety and healthy intimacy. A caring partner can help them get over lingering effects such as possible sexual dysfunction and emotional triggers.

How the Degree of Closeness in the Relationship Between the Abused and Abuser Changes the Long-Term Effects

Generally, a child will be more traumatized by sexual abuse when he is close emotionally to the abuser than when he doesn't know the perpetrator very well. If abuse occurs within a close relationship, the child feels a greater sense of betrayal and the breaking of an important trust.

Case notes: *Allen, age 11, admired and trusted his parish priest. Allen didn't have a living father so an emotional attachment was made to the priest as a substitute father. Allen's trust was destroyed when the priest masturbated in his presence several times. Allen felt betrayal because the priest defied religious standards and practices as well as societal taboos. Allen's self-respect was also decreased because the priest found him sexually attractive. If Allen had been physically touched by a stranger, he would most likely not have been as seriously affected as he was when a trusted person subjected him to abuse, even without touching him.*

Actual physical contact is often less serious than the violation of trust and appropriate boundaries.

How Touching and Violence Change Long-Term Effects

Physically violent sexual abuse can be extremely traumatic because the child is not only being violated but also will develop a fear of death. This multiplies the trauma.

Case notes: *Mary, age 12, was raped while walking home from school by someone she had never seen. The perpetrator compelled her to cooperate by screaming, "Give me what I want or you die!" For years after, she suffered from nightmares of the incident because of the threats to kill her if she didn't cooperate.*

The greater the force and violence involved in an abuse case, the greater the negative effects on the victim. Painful and sadistic treatment is far more traumatic than abuse which resembles gentle, caring affection. Verbal abuse and consequent humiliation often accompany rape. They can be more damaging than the physical act itself.

When a perpetrator actually touches a child, the child is more likely to be more disturbed than if the abuser does not. For instance, exhibitionism generally does not have the impact that fondling does, unless, of course, the abuser is close emotionally to the child. Likewise, fondling may be less disturbing than actual intercourse. A victim tends to blame himself and is blamed more by others if there is actual touching.

How the Time Frame of the Abuse Affects the Degree of Trauma

Sexual abuse tends to be more disturbing if it goes on over a long period of time rather than consisting of a single incident. The re-victimization that accompanies repetitive abuse seems to compound the feelings of shame and guilt.

Case notes: *Peggy, age 28, was sexually abused during most of her adolescence by her sister's husband who was 20 years older than she. Peggy felt like both the betrayer (of her sister) and the betrayed (by her sister's husband). She felt her sister would be crushed emotionally if she knew, so Peggy is still keeping the secret even though the abuse stopped several years ago. This victimization was traumatic and damaging. When Peggy was 11 years old, one of her male teachers in school touched her breast. She never told anyone about this incident either. Although the experience with the teacher was painful, she doesn't feel it contributed as much as the experience with the brother-in-law, to her emotionally shaky state of mind today.*

The Amount of Affection Between the Victim and Perpetrator Affects Trauma

Generally, if the abuse is not violent and is based on at least some degree of affection, the victim has a better chance to escape the worst emotional trauma. An exception is long-term incest where the feeling of betrayal far outweighs other variables. Being used or exploited the way a pimp exploits a prostitute can be very damaging.

Case notes: *Rose's father sexually abused her for several years. Rose is intellectually disabled. Not only did her father have sexual intercourse with her over a long period of time, but she was also intermittently used by her grandfather and brother. The feeling of exploitation was even further compounded when the father brought two of his friends from work home to use Rose sexually on several occasions. Rose has grown up to require placement in a mental health group home. She must be closely supervised as she tries to sexually abuse children as she once was abused. She has girl and boy dolls which she physically positions as if they are having sexual experiences together.*

How the Gender of the Perpetrator Affects Trauma

The fact that sexual abuse comes from a person of the same sex can be a factor in the degree of trauma. Victims of homosexual abuse can have sexual identity problems as adults.

Case notes: *Charlie, age 32, was sexually abused by the carpenter who came to remodel his family's home when he was 13 years old. Charlie got to know the carpenter and came to admire him as a friend. Charlie was used as a female when rectal intercourse was performed with him. He has grown up with a sexual dysfunction (he cannot get an erection when in a sexual situation with a woman). This is because he doubts his masculinity and, as a result, has anxiety about performing sexually.*

Society accepts sexual abuse of a female more readily than that of a male. Male sexual abuse is more secretive and, so, is less often revealed. One of the reasons that a male survivor is more likely to suffer trauma is that he is less likely to have revealed and resolved the abuse. If a man has been sexually abused as a child by another male, he has broken both the sexual taboo and the homosexual taboo. This is an unbearable combination to him. The male victim may label himself as a homosexual because he has not only submitted to a homosexual experience but because he has been found sexually attractive by another male. He can label himself as homosexual and, therefore, behaves in accordance with a homosexual role and gravitates toward same-sex activity.

A boy who has been sexually abused by an older male has a great chance of engaging in homosexual acts when he becomes an adult, especially if he does not obtain therapy or resolve the issues raised by the abuse. Sexual activity with a much older male will break a boy's faith in the generation on which he is basically emotionally dependent. Sexual experiences with another male who is around the same age are generally far less traumatic than those involving an adult because generational lines are not crossed. Many adolescent boys experiment sexually with each other as part of growing up without later preferring male sexual partners.

How Prior Sexual Experience Affects Trauma

If a young person has had a prior sexual experience which was good, he is less likely to be traumatized than if it is a first sexual experience.

Case notes: *Monica, age 34, was sexually abused by an out of town friend of the family when she was 16 years old. He came into her bedroom (he was staying with the family), put his hand over her mouth and raped her. Monica never told her parents as she felt ashamed and feared her parents would not believe her since the friend and her parents had a long-standing relationship. She was hurt and humiliated. However, she had a sexual relationship with her boyfriend, Don, at the time the rape occurred. Monica feels she suffered less ill-effects because she knew sex could be a beautiful, sharing experience before the brutal rape happened.*

The Long-Term Effects of Abuse

There are many adult men and women who are carrying around the pain of being sexually abused as children. They may be said to suffer from the "victimization syndrome." Because these people view themselves as "victims" rather than "survivors," they live their lives being sexually, emotionally, and/or physically victimized. Victimization is almost a certainty when the individual has felt years of anger and guilt in connection with the abuse.

Guilt and low self-esteem promote victimization. Society condemns sexual abuse and, as a result, the victim often blames himself for doing something "bad" and participating, even if he was coerced, bribed or threatened. The blame of self is turned into guilt and a feeling of worthlessness which in turn leads to low self esteem. A person who feels he has little worth does not feel he has the right to stand up for himself and gets taken advantage of and victimized over and over. Because of the exploitive nature of the abuse, the survivor is angry both about being used and about having no one to protect him from being victimized. The anger is turned in on himself and a depression can set in which accompanies the low self-esteem. The survivor feels unloved. There is a feeling of hopelessness and of being "tainted" or "dirty." The survivor, as a result, sets himself up to be punished over and over by being victimized. He feels he needs to be punished even though the abuse is painful and debilitating. Sexual abuse survivors often have what is called a "repetition compulsion," i.e., a strong need to repeat the abusive relationship as a way of punishing themselves. The destructive self-victimization is endlessly repeated.

Case notes: *Donna, age 45, was in therapy to improve her self-esteem and learn how to stop being "treated as a doormat." She had almost no personal boundaries, and found herself being verbally abused by coworkers, people at her church, and even her young nieces and nephews. She came to realize that her natural sense of herself as a person had been severely damaged as a child when she endured years of off-and-on sexual abuse by a neighbor. She said her primary personal boundary had been perforated—like a protective wall with hundreds of holes, she had no way to feel strong or safe.*

The normal adult mechanism of self protection is impaired by low self image. Because the victim has a debased self image, both men and women can end up being victimized repeatedly. There can be a feeling of deserving punishment and actually going out and seeking it, or it can be sought unconsciously. If the parents of the survivor blamed the abuse on him because they felt impotent in dealing with the abuse, he is likely to have a greater sense of guilt and self-blame.

Survivors are frequently rape victims because they put themselves into potentially dangerous situations. For instance, they may not take proper precautions about walking around at night, being picked up at bars and going home with a stranger, getting into a car with someone they don't know, etc.

Case notes: *Debbie, age 28, has been raped three times in the last nine years after being sexually abused as a child on frequent occasions by her mother's boyfriend. The first rape occurred when she was 15 as she was being interviewed for a job. Her potential boss kept her in his office past the closing time for the business even though the interview had already lasted for over an hour. Instead of thanking the man for the interview and leaving when the employees left, Debbie stayed. She did not leave though sexual innuendos began to appear in the man's conversation. Finally, he raped her brutally. Debbie felt powerless, and told no one. Her victim mentality continued to affect her life. The other two rapes occurred when she was 23 and 26 years of age. Both happened as she was walking home alone at night through city streets. One of these rapes was carried out by a gang of boys who hung out in her neighborhood.*

Sexual Difficulties

Because of the sexual abuse, there is confusion between sex and affection in the mind of the survivor. He has learned to relate sexually and makes sexual overtures toward a potential partner even if he only really wants affection and nurturance. The survivor feels valued for his or her body alone and may act seductive to get attention and privileges.

Case notes: *Kathy, age 15, was placed in foster care when it was discovered she had been sexually abused for a number of years by her stepfather. On one occasion when the foster father told Kathy she could not go out, she began unbuttoning her blouse. She had become conditioned to getting what she wanted by being seductive and sexual. She frequently tried to sit in the foster father's lap as she had become used to receiving affection and attention only when she was acting sexual.*

Prostitutes often come from sexually abusive childhoods. These men and women feel "tainted" and good for only one thing, i.e., serving another person sexually.

There are many parallels in the behavior of other survivors. For example: Survivors often grow up to have sexual dysfunctions and/or sexual relationships which are not enjoyable. They may be unable to distinguish between sex and affection and this may show up as either sexual dysfunction or promiscuity. There is frequently a denial of sexual desire as the victim feels "dirty." Sex is frequently perceived as "disgusting." There is a negative sexual identification, such as "I'm not sexually appealing." There is little pride in being a man or a woman. The guilt survivors feel about their sexuality leads, ultimately, to ambivalent feelings about their relationships. A relationship may offer necessary love and security, yet prove to be disappointing or even painful.

Sexual relationships are often masochistic since the survivor tends to work himself into a position where he relives past abuse which hurt and humiliated him. Survivors often expect to be exploited and so become exploited.

Angry survivors often position themselves to be rape victims or become rapists. Childhood sexual abuse causes the survivor to feel powerless and out of control. Raping or otherwise sexually abusing others (adopting the role of the perpetrator) is one way for some survivors to feel control and power. A "sinner script," which is the identification of one's self as a bad person, can cause the anger to come out in subtle ways. For example:

Case notes: *Marsha, age 37, relates: I lead men on. I tease them and get them all sexually excited and hot for me and then I withdraw. I love to hear them beg for my body as I walk away. Sometimes I do go to bed with one of them and try to get him to like me. Just when he is aroused, I turn him off. I feel in control when a guy is all crazy about me. I know I have him right where I want him...I'm in control of him and at the time no longer feel like a victim. The revenge I'm getting is meant for all those men who have victimized me.*

Survivors, such as Marsha, feel permanently stigmatized as if a "whore inside." They feel like sexual objects who have nothing more to offer than their bodies.

"Objectification is the root of evil," a colleague of mine said. First, a child or adult is treated inhumanely, i.e., as an object instead of a human being. He or she is used only for the gratification of the abuser with no consideration for how the experience is harming the victim. The perpetrator stops seeing the child or other person with any empathy, only as an object to be exploited. Unfortunately, that victim can later start to objectify other people and exploit them in similar ways that are all too familiar.

A key step in shifting to "survivor" from "victim" is when the abused person reclaims his or her humanity and starts to treat themselves and others as people who deserve respect and appreciation for who they are as a person, not as a sex object.

Problems with Lover/Spouses

Because these survivors have been profoundly betrayed, they learn to expect abuse, exploitation and disappointment in future relationships. Some of the attitudes we humans have about ourselves become self-fulfilling prophecies. Survivors tend to get what they expect, i.e., exploitation. Because of victims' expectations and distrust, they often choose partners who are untrustworthy and unreliable.

Case notes: *Mary, a childhood sexual abuse survivor, age 42, complained bitterly to me that "all men are animals" and that they are "out for all they can get." Her latest male friend steals money from her purse and runs around with other women. He lies about where he is going and generally treats her with little respect. As a typical survivor, she believes she cannot get affection without offering sex. So, she offers him sex as often as he wants it in spite of the many ways he mistreats her. Mary's friend has proven to her that she should not trust him. Once again, she is "right about men."*

Lack of trust is a typical feature of such cases. Because of the distrust, the victim feels his partner is just going to use him anyway. So there is a holding back of feeling and genuine communication. This in turn prevents closeness in a cycle which the survivors must strive to break.

Case notes: *Bob, age 32, was sexually abused by a male relative as a child. He is in a gay relationship with a man who really does value Bob as a person. Bob doesn't believe anyone would not want to use him so he keeps himself at a distance emotionally. Bob has finally found someone who cares, but he does not accept the caring psychologically. He feels he cannot possibly deserve such caring; thus, he also cannot believe it is part of a sincere and lasting relationship.*

Problems with Parenting

Often, sexually abused parents also fail to protect their children. Survivors frequently choose sexually abusive partners who batter them. They may not protect their own children from abuse, perhaps because abuse was an accepted pattern when they were growing up and because their parents related to them in similar fashion, giving little protection.

Victims can turn out to be either the abusive parent or the non-abusive parent. The non-abusive parent who is the victim in the relationship does not like his or her children being abused but, since it's something so familiar, may not fight aggressively to stop it. A person who has been abused is much more likely to abuse his own children, or to tolerate their children being abused.

The Super-Mom Syndrome

Compulsive caretaking is one way women who feel worthless as a result of victimization abuse themselves. For instance, some survivors grow up to be super-moms who knock themselves out for their children. Super-moms feel resentful toward their children even when they ask not to be catered to. These women often have grown up with a mother who did not teach them good mothering. Their natural instincts make them overcompensate. They are self-sacrificing while hating themselves for being so. Being a "martyr" is the flip side of being a "victim," and some survivors go back and forth.

Problems with Friendships

The survivor frequently feels lonely and isolated from others because of the feelings of degradation and shame. There is a feeling of being "different" and of being "damaged goods."

Case notes: *Pattie, age 28, was involved in an incestuous relationship with an uncle who raised her. The abuse continued from ages 12 to 18. Uncle George insisted she not have any friends as he wanted her to himself. She felt isolated and alone and felt very bad when she could not attend her Senior Prom at school because her uncle wouldn't let her go. She wanted to be like the other girls, yet she was ashamed of her sexual relationship with her uncle and didn't want anyone to find out about it. She kept to herself at school so no one would find out her secret, and of course never asked a friend to come over to her uncle's home where she lived. When Pattie became an adult, she still felt degraded and didn't have the confidence to make friends. She had not developed the necessary social skills to relate to others her own age.*

Men and women who have been sexually abused often have difficulty having a sense of themselves because they have been so overpowered, and have had almost no control over their lives. They have a difficult time describing their attributes or just generally answering the question, "Who am I?" They find relating to either a man or a woman very difficult because a mature relationship requires knowledge and self-confidence they have not had the opportunity to develop.

The victim learns to act seductively toward the perpetrator; he in turn is possessive about the victim, as the abuse goes on over a long period of time. In this way, the individual stops growing socially and emotionally at the time the abuse begins. Children who are forced to go on with the abusive relationships into adulthood usually get stuck in emotional adolescence for a long time after becoming adults. The adult survivor may still be rebellious, buck authority, and be casting around for self-identity as teenagers do. This creates a brazen image that is distinctly unattractive to mature adults and leaves the victim without any chance to appeal to a partner who could rescue him from the cycle of abuse.

Women incest victims of father/daughter relationships often identify with their all-powerful father and perceive their mothers as worthless. This leads to still another problem with friendships. They are angry at their mothers for not protecting them from abuse and carry this anger over to all women. Men who are overvalued in their relationships with women are often shallow and emotionally meaningless. As a result, they are often unable to establish a close, supportive relationship with another woman—something they desperately need.

Self-Destructive Behavior

The survivor is endlessly searching for nurturance and belonging. He is trying to find a caretaker yet doesn't feel he deserves being taken care of. He feels lonely and in pain and often tries to blot out these feelings with excessive alcohol or drug use. It has been my experience that a large number of battered wives have a history of sexual abuse as children. They are sometimes alcoholics or are addicted to drugs. According to recent studies, it is estimated that between 54%-74% of all alcoholics have been sexually abused as children at least once. Other studies reveal that between 44%-53% who were admitted to alcohol rehabilitation centers had been sexually abused.

Alcohol is used to reduce the survivor's feelings of shame, guilt, anger, and low self-esteem. Younger survivors use drugs and/or alcohol to accomplish the same purpose.

In addition, there is a very specific relationship between incest and alcoholism. Many incest survivors have sexual impediments as a result of the abuse they have experienced. Studies conclude that most incestuous fathers were under the influence of alcohol when they abused their sons or daughters. Thus, the survivor grows up believing that alcohol can overcome his sexual impediments. Survivors of incestuous fathers who drink also run a greater risk of becoming an alcoholic because of genetic factors.

Those survivors who cannot take the pain of their existence at home and run away often end up as prostitutes or find work in pornography to support themselves on the street. Some people are not disposed to medicate their emotional pain by using alcohol or drugs, but turn to other forms of addictive behaviors; these include overeating, bulimia, anorexia, compulsive spending or gambling, sex, and romantic fantasy. Others avoid feelings and painful memories by becoming workaholics.

A more drastic reaction to the pain of being a survivor is suicide. Some experience a psychotic break which will require psychiatric hospitalization either temporarily or on a long-term basis. Survivors can turn to these "escapes" if they are not helped to deal with the sexual abuse experience.

If a survivor was abused by a stranger in a violent way, such as rape, he often will develop a fear of the unknown and will view the world as a dangerous place. He can become chronically fearful and apprehensive and not only physically isolated, but cut off emotionally from friends or other supporters.

Adding to the distrust of people and hampering relationships are events which occurred if the abuse was discovered when the survivor was a child. Some survivors have experienced leers, lewd remarks, and come-ons and have been thereby ostracized from their peer groups.

Sexual Harassment in the Workplace

Survivors are also victimized at work by those who sexually harass them. Sexual harassment is a physical or verbal sexual advance that is not desired. It may take the form of either a demand or a strong request. The most extreme form of sexual harassment is a situation where the perpetrator implies that sexual responsiveness is a required condition of employment. More common harassment involves the sale of pay raises and promotions for sexual favors. It may also take on a more subtle form, in which there is no direct link to specific rewards, but the survivor is nevertheless made to feel like a victim. This inevitably results in an offensive work environment for the victim, and, in the vast majority of cases, reduced productivity in their work. Employees who are being sexually harassed are expected to give in and never complain . The sexual harassment usually does not end unless the victim chooses to end the victimization by speaking up and being assertive. Fortunately, it is possible with all of the changes in the law that indeed you do not have to live or work with being sexually harassed or sexually assaulted. If you wish to take action on your sexual harassment, there are laws that will protect you and procedures to report it and get legal help. It is fortunate, that with the growth of the Me, Too movement, you now have women to follow who have bravely brought attention to the vastness of sexual harassment and abuse by those in power by reporting it publicly. You have much more support than ever before.

Acquaintance Rape

Acquaintance rape or date rape is just beginning to be recognized as a common form of sexual abuse and a major national issue. This is a rape involving both someone the victim knows and conditions of voluntary association. The victim has willingly gone out on a date with the potential rapist and often has gone to his home or invited him to her home willingly. The victim feels she won't be believed if she reports the rape. Because of her initial trust in the perpetrator, she is sure a jury would suspect she is lying about his behavior. As a result, she doesn't report the incident and the perpetrator can go on to treat others similarly. Surveys of college campuses (Cornell University, University of South Dakota, and North Carolina State University) estimate the incident of "acquaintance rape" to be one in four or five college students. (These victims are often survivors who choose to go out with someone who they unconsciously perceive as a victim.)

When the rape occurs, they follow their old established patterns of blaming themselves and experiencing guilt. Survivors are especially vulnerable to a date rapist who has a talent for spotting a woman who may be vulnerable to victimization. He is not a typical rapist. He wines and dines his victim and seriously believes she "owes" him sexual cooperation in return. These men are often charming and not necessarily the "macho" type. The rapist is a repeat offender who will continue this behavior until he is stopped. Since most women will not report the rape because of a fear of not being believed and self-blame, he is able to victimize innumerable women.

These victimizers can almost always be stopped in their tracks if the woman says "no" forcefully. Unfortunately, preyed-upon women often feel they deserve to be victimized, or may become inexplicably confused and will not protect themselves. If a woman does deter the aggressor's advances, he merely moves on to another one who will submit, one who feels like a victim, one who has little self-worth, and one who is not assertive.

Although the victimizer does seem to obtain sexual gratification, his main motive in raping a date is to wield his power over a woman. A woman survivor has a better chance of avoiding a potential date rapist if she knows to look for certain signs. Does he seem to be accustomed to using violence or force to achieve his goals? Does he refer to abuse within his own family (meaning he may have learned to abuse)? He usually has a history of short, uncommitted relationships and, underneath the charming exterior, harbors enormous anger. He directs this anger at any available woman. He does not view himself as a rapist, but as someone who is getting the "rewards" he deserves.

Marital Rape

Marital rape is another example of a survivor getting herself attached to a potential abuser. These people expect others to exploit them and often choose relationships and even marriages that are sexually abusive. Greta is a typical case.

Case notes: *Greta, age 54, is beaten and battered by her alcoholic husband at least once a month. After he beats her, he likes to have sex with her as she struggles to get out of his grasp. Because she is weak from the battering, she doesn't have much strength to fight back and he subjects her to a painful rape.*

INCEST

Incest survivors have not only the aforementioned symptoms of sexual abuse but additional emotional scars as well. Incest is most often the most damaging of all sexual abuse because of vast betrayal by someone the child loves and trusts to protect him. The feelings of guilt, anger, loss of self-esteem, exploitation, and helplessness are magnified in the incest survivor.

Mother/Son Incest

The effects of mother/son incest can be tremendously damaging and devastating, often robbing the son of any kind of fulfilling future. The long term effects are caused by the mother's over-protectiveness and her overly-demanding attitude toward him. The victim becomes insecure and often grows up to be a loner incapable of establishing a relationship with a woman his own age. A long-term mother/son incestuous situation can actually result in the man's being able to have a sexual relationship only with his mother.

The sons of such relationships may leave their mothers physically but not emotionally. They remain very attached to their mothers in the psychological sense and suffer inadequate relationships with either sex. Some never leave home or may leave and return home because emotionally they are married to their mothers. This may occur even though they have experienced no intercourse or sexually specific behavior. The mother's sexually stimulating actions may have consisted of sleeping with her son or dressing and bathing him beyond the appropriate age.

His trust in women is low because of the mother's betrayal and his sexual identity is a problem for him since he has most likely not had a strong relationship with his father, if any, in the home.

Children need a same-sex role model to learn how to be a man or woman.

Case notes: *Greg, age 42, was never married. However, he has lived with several women since he first left home at age 24. During the live-in experiences, he was very unhappy with the women, constantly comparing them unfavorably to his mother. Because he lived some distance away from his mother, it was not always possible to spend holidays like Thanksgiving and Christmas with her. On these holidays he would berate the current live-in woman, telling her she didn't know how to make a good holiday like his mother. Then he would proceed to get "sick" and take to his bed under the covers for the holiday.*

When Greg was growing up, his mother was extremely protective and suffocating emotionally. She referred to him as her "number one" and convinced him that only she could make him happy by fawning over him. The strong emotional attachment caused Greg to be a loner who had few friends as a child. No one, he felt, could provide him with emotional strokes like his mother. Even though there was no explicit sexual activity between them, Greg was seduced emotionally by her. Greg's father was emotionally distant from his son and when Greg reached adolescence, a raging conflict between the two of them surfaced. Although their verbal battles did not deal specifically with who was in possession of the mother emotionally, that was the underlying issue.

When Greg introduced his various women friends to his mother, she would be superficially nice to them. When speaking to Greg alone, she would be critical of them, acting as if she was in competition for her son. Greg fell into a pattern of physically and emotionally battering women who could not measure up to his idealized view of his mother.

Greg has moved back into his mother's home and has no friends, either male or female. He no longer works and in essence, has regressed back to his childhood in terms of his physical behavior. Emotionally, he never left. The implicitly seductive relationship continues. His mother washes his clothes, cooks his meals, picks up after him and takes physical care of the unfortunate boy/man she has created.

"Greg" is also an example of emotional incest. See the material under *Emotional Incest* later in this chapter. The son in mother/son incest really ends up taking emotional care of his mother since she is keeping him close to her to fulfill *her* needs, not his.

Brother/Sister Incest

Brother/sister incest is probably the least damaging of incestuous relationships since it does not cross generational boundaries, i.e., both participants are around the same age and neither (usually) depends on the other for protection and parenting.

For a girl, if the parents discover the incest and her mother or father blames her for it, the daughter's chances of emotional damage are increased. The girl typically accepts the blame and feels guilty, depressed, and shameful. Even if it is not discovered, the survivor of this kind of incest often is emotionally damaged, particularly if the brother forces his sister to submit sexually. Because of culture "norms," the boy may feel that at least he "is not a virgin," justifying his assault or seduction of the easy target in his own home, whereas the girl may feel "robbed" of her virginity, ashamed, and "ruined."

Note that if children in your home are found engaging in any type of sexual behavior, whether they are siblings, cousins, or just friends, you must ask yourself if one of the children "learned" the behavior from an adult—from someone who has abused them. If you don't feel you can calmly and competently investigate this possibility, make an appointment with a mental health professional who can talk with the child or children in a safe setting to discover what secrets need to be uncovered. Do not think there is a 100% chance the child had been abused, but there is a strong possibility which must not be stepped over.

Father/Son Incest

Keeping in mind that the majority of people are heterosexual, and abuse that forces homosexual experiences on boys and girls can have severe and long-term psychological effects.

The consequences of father/son incest can be very serious and long-lasting, especially since it breaks not only the sexual abuse taboo, but also violates the taboo regarding homosexuality.

The son questions his masculinity since he is engaged in sex with another male and can feel dirty, worthless, and guilty. To repress the stress caused by this type of incest, the boy may turn to excessive drug and/or alcohol use. Since he feels like "damaged goods" he may become socially isolated. This type of incest occurs because heterosexual men who were sexually abused by their own fathers do not learn how to have a well-balanced relationship with a woman. They may then turn to their own sons for sexual satisfaction. For this reason, father/son incest is perpetuated through several generations if there is not intervention.

Case notes: *Nate, age 16, recently confided to his school counselor that his father has been sodomizing (having anal intercourse) with him since he was eight years old. The abuse was reported to authorities and, upon further investigation, it was discovered that Nate's father had been sexually abused by his father. Nate is getting professional help and hopefully this vicious circle of father/son incest will be broken.*

Survivors of father/son incest may grow up to be prostitutes for other men. Many survivors who have sex for money are trying to find the nurturing and protection they missed as a child from a "daddy." To say they are confused about their own sexual identity is an understatement. The man may not feel that he is homosexual, yet finds himself compelled to seek out men in his empty efforts to experience a satisfying connection with a man.

Case notes: *Jim, age 32, is a male prostitute. He goes home with various men he picks up in gay bars. He is used and then at times physically or emotionally discarded. What Jim really wants is a lover to take care of him and love him.*

Emotional Incest

Some survivors of sexual abuse are the victims of "emotional incest" as youngsters. Even if there is no sexual contact, the relationship is sexualized, i.e., the parent is seductive and there is a strong emotional bond between the parent and child which excludes other adults, brothers, or sisters. The relationship is more like an intimate peer relationship. Victims of emotional incest frequently grow up to exhibit the same effects as survivors because of the emotional suffocation.

A nine-year old girl who lived with her (divorced) mother complained to her father during a visitation: "Mom treats me like such a baby. She still makes me take bubble baths with her every night." Later, in a custody hearing, it also came out that the girl was often kept home from school to keep her mother company. A judge labeled that mother's behavior "emotional incest."

GETTING PROFESSIONAL HELP
FOR THE SURVIVOR

Why it is Necessary to Get Help

Because the sexual abuse taboo is starting to crumble, survivors feel they can admit abuse and can seek help more freely. Effects can be corrected and changed and the survivor can proceed to live a happy, fulfilling life.

It is necessary for survivors to resolve the issues of anger, blame, guilt, and other feelings engendered by the abuse in therapy, thereby enabling them to give up their roles as self-destructive victims. Clients are often unaware of the effect the abuse has on their behavior. They need to know that sexual victimization may be at the root of many problems which are listed at the end of this chapter. Resolving abuse issues will help relieve any ensuing problems.

A good therapist helps the client understand that anger toward the perpetrator is often transferred to all the individuals who are of the same sex as the perpetrator. For instance, a female survivor may feel anger at all men. Although she may need the nurturance and caring of a male relationship, she repels men who are able to fulfill her needs. Because of her anger, she may not be able to attract a man, or she may attract only those men who are themselves angry and are therefore attracted to angry women. A relationship based on mutual anger from the past can be agonizing and painful for the participants as they are usually angry with each other. As the client's anger is resolved, he is able to create newer and healthier relationships.

Unfortunately, a victim who has not had help to heal and resolve past abuse issues rarely develops a healthy, lasting, intimate relationship. If it's not anger getting in the way, it can simply be naivety. They do not understand what healthy boundaries are (how would they?) nor how to discern who is a healthy, safe person to get involved with. The familiarity of being dominated and/or abused becomes part of a pattern where the victim repeats their past, or sometimes flips it so that he or she becomes the abuser instead of the victim. But they still remain a victim, robbed of their chance of a functional life and healthy relationships. Everyone deserves a chance to heal, and should have access to those who are qualified to help.

Finding a Therapist

Professional help is available almost everywhere. The client needs to find a therapist who is experienced in dealing with the dynamics of sexual abuse who therefore won't be shocked or critical of what they reveal. Often, survivors don't obtain help because they feel guilty or shameful or fear a negative reaction. Therapists who react negatively only reinforce these feelings. A negative reaction tells the client that he is indeed a shameful and undesirable person. Because of his position of power and authority, a therapist can absolutely demolish a survivor's self-esteem, which is already shaky, with a reaction that is anything less than supportive and accepting.

The Content of the Therapy

The therapist's focus needs to center on improving the client's self-image and working through the old persistent feelings of anger and guilt. People who feel guilty tend to punish themselves by recreating the situation which caused the guilt in the first place. If this feature of the survivor's behavior is not addressed, he will continue to play out a victim's script. The therapist must teach the survivor that the abuse was 100% the fault of the perpetrator. The offender is always the guilty party, not the survivor. A child victim has no knowledge of what is sexually expected of him and is completely unable to consent to the abuse knowledgeably. If the survivor is married, the couple often requires marital therapy to resolve issues caused by past sexual abuse which may be hampering the relationship, including sexual dysfunction. Survivors may block sexual abuse completely out of their minds and "forget" it because the experience was so painful. Sometimes a client will go to psychotherapy for reasons other than sexual abuse and flash back and slowly start remembering.

Case notes: *Jeanette, age 43, came into therapy because she was depressed about breaking up with her live-in lover of three years. As we discussed her childhood, it was discovered that she had "forgotten" almost all of her childhood years from 8 to 12 years of age. As Jeanette began to trust me, she felt safe enough to remember that her foster father had abused her during the three missing years. We worked through her pain and she eventually was able to begin resolving the effects of her victimization once the experience was out in the open.*

When memories begin to surface the survivor goes through a period of denial: "It didn't happen to me." The therapist must allow the client to fully recognize the abuse and work on the disclosure in his own time. The survivor, whether married or not, needs to learn that a sexual relationship can be positive and that being sexual is an integral part of a person. The victim learns to become responsible for his own sexuality, i.e. it is his choice whether to participate in sex and sexual encounters may b e planned. The power of how a person's sexual life is conducted is returned to the survivor and, hence, the person ceases to view sexuality as out of his control.

The most important concept that the survivor must believe and understand is that sexual experiences enhance an individual's life, rather than causing trouble and anguish. A therapist who has a positive outlook on sexuality can be a powerful role model for the client. It is necessary for the survivor to accept the reality of the sexual abuse and not deny that it happened. They are not to blame and need to express regrets that it happened.

There is a difference between things in our lives that are changeable and things that are unchangeable. We cannot change the past, so it must be accepted. We can change behavior patterns learned in the past. A survivor is indeed a survivor in the truest sense of the word. The client needs to realize and take pride in the fact that he has coped with and survived a very damaging experience since childhood and has dealt with all the problems it created. He needs to be told to take pride in his ability to survive.

Assertiveness skills are taught which further reduce the chance of further victimization. Self-protective skills are taught by covering such subjects as reducing sexual victimization on the street, in a car, in the home, and on dates. Survivors have so often ignored safety issues because of unconscious desires to punish themselves that it becomes necessary to educate them in these areas. Clients who drink excessively learn control of an alcohol consumption problem if drinking leads them into a potentially dangerous situation, such as being raped. Alcohol and drugs are dis-inhibitors which help set the stage for further victimization because the survivor's defenses are lowered even further than usual. He is taught how to choose a partner who will help him create a healthy relationship. The criteria are:

1. He is comfortable with the person;

2. There is an attraction to the potential partner;

3. The other person must respect and work with him. He will not punish or try to control him.

Male survivors present a special challenge for therapists as they not only have the women's effects from sexual abuse but also are likely to sexually abuse others if they are not treated. Most often a perpetrator is motivated by anger and a sense of powerlessness in his life. He has the need to dominate another person by hurting and degrading that person, especially perpetrators who forcibly abuse others. Since about 90% of perpetrators are males, it is extremely important for the survivor to gain a sense of power and control of his life without victimizing others to obtain these feelings. Males gain a sense of confidence through assigned tasks and accomplishments which serve as exercises that permit them to practice control of their lives. Skills are taught and tasks are carried out and mastered. In other words, he learns to view himself as a more adequate human being.

Survivors need to understand that therapy and dealing with sexual abuse issues feels good sometimes and at other times feels painful. Healing emotionally takes time and patience and may involve much pain.

THE CHARACTERISTICS OF GROUP THERAPY

Group therapy is an effective method of helping survivors resolve their difficulties in life which have been caused by childhood sexual abuse.

One reason group therapy works is that the members of the group can grant each other absolution. Since survivors often feel like "sinners," it is important for them to forgive themselves and not to feel blame. This self-forgiveness happens more easily when a group member looks around at the others and thinks of the fact that they were not to blame for their being abused; he learns that others view him in the same way, i.e. not to blame. This form of therapy also works because the group members feel stronger helping each other than they would alone. This assists them in not feeling so much like victims. This "terrible secret" is shared, which reduces a feeling of isolation from others. Sharing the secret is so important that many group members feel greatly relieved in doing so. Through the sharing comes self-acceptance and a cessation of guilt and self-blame. Often heard in support groups is the assertion, "You are only as sick as your secrets." Group members encourage one another to share the unsharable, to finally let go of self-harming secrets in an environment that is non-judgmental, safe, and accepting. It is also important for the survivors to eventually share the secrets with someone outside of the group to further promote emotional healing and to lessen the feelings of shame.

Assertiveness is often missing in survivors. In the group, members can practice being assertive with one another in this relatively sheltered environment before going outside of the group. Very often, graduates from the survivors' groups go on to work with victims in rape centers, battered women's shelters, and other organizations. Some survivors learn to confront perpetrators in these organizations.

This can be a valuable experience, but only if the survivor is strong enough to deal with a perpetrator's denial that it even happened or accusations that the survivor is crazy. Perpetrators can be defensive or will attack in response to the confrontation. However, if the survivor can handle it, there is a great deal of strength to be gained from releasing the feeling produced by the sexual abuse to another, inevitably similar perpetrator. Releasing old anger or other feelings is the first step in building a new life.

SIGNS A TRAINED PROFESSIONAL NOTICES

Survivors have many personality traits that are directly related, psychologically, to their abuse they have endured. An individual will typically have most or all of these characteristics.

146

1. **Unfulfilling Relationships with Others**

   - Because trust in human beings in general has been betrayed, survivors experience difficulty in being close to others. There is a fear of being vulnerable and open to hurt. Many choose partners or friends who are distant because they fear intimacy. This is a form of emotional protection.

   - In the incidence of incest, the survivor may also experience shallow relationships with those of their own sex. A woman may feel angry at her mother for not protecting her and transfer this bitterness onto all women.

   - Because of the social isolation, especially in incest relationships, the survivor has not learned to have social relationships with people their own age. If they do have social relationships, their friends are often older.

   - Survivors often choose a romantic partner or friends who are abusive and who will continue victimizing the survivor.

2. **Sexual Difficulties**

   - Association of affection with sex. The survivor may have learned to relate sexually even when only nurturance is needed.

   - Many survivors have learned that sex is the response to a stimulus—i.e., a privilege offered by a parent. Survivors may be unable to respond sexually or to avoid sex altogether because of guilt and shame about the sexual impulses and a denial of femininity/masculinity which in a few instances may lead a person to view themselves as homosexual. Sometimes during sex the survivor may have "flashbacks" which inhibit response.

   - Sometimes the conflict between sex and caring is acted out in such a way that the survivor is unable to have sex in an intimate relationship while retaining the ability to have sex with strangers. This is a way of acting out anger. The survivor can have many such sexual relationships. Survivors' behaviors range from the extreme of never being the sexual aggressor to being the aggressor all the time.

3. **Disregard For One's Body**

   - Some survivors abuse their bodies. Getting fat can be a way to avoid sexual attention. Wearing baggy clothes or excessive clothing, even in the summer, can be another way. Survivors may be accident-prone as a way of punishing their bodies and may even mutilate themselves. Eating disorders such as bulimia or anorexia are sometimes experienced.

4. **Somatic Complaints**

   - There can be problems with the reproductive organs, head or backaches, joint aches or other physical difficulties. Sleep disturbances or night terrors can occur.

5. **Alcohol or Drug Problems or Addiction**

   - Substances are used to blot out loneliness and emotional pain.

6. **Control Issues**

   - Survivors feel out of control and without power. They may not be able to take control as a parent and may be passive-aggressive (non-assertive) in personal relationships. That is, they may submit to aggressiveness in another, or they may try to overcompensate for feelings of powerlessness by being super-aggressive and controlling.

7. **Depression**

   - There is a sadness and a non-responsiveness to the world and their own feelings. They may not feel entitled to happiness or may even believe they deserve to be hurt. Suicidal thoughts, attempts or obsessions may be present along with crying.

8. **Anger**

   - A survivor may be angry all the time or may "blow up" at trivial incidents as a result of pent-up anger. There may be an intense hostility towards those who are the same gender or race as the perpetrator. Pent-p anger must be expressed gradually in therapy.

9. **The Damaged Goods Syndrome**

   - Survivors may feel like used merchandise and may refer to themselves as "whores," "bitches" or "scum." There is a feeling of being tainted, worthless, evil and beyond redemption. They feel marked and different from others. As a way of compensating, they they expect themselves to be perfect.

10. **Denial of Abuse**

    - Some survivors may not remember the abuse at all. They may have gaps in their memories about the years of victimization and become amnesic. Especially indicative of possible abuse is the blocking out of some period of years between 6-12 years of age. Certain life events can jog the survivor's memory such as therapy, the birth of his or her own child, or the death of the perpetrator. Some survivors minimize the effects of the abuse, i.e. "It wasn't all that bad" as a defense against feeling the pain and related feelings.

11. **Victimization Syndrome**

    - Survivors have life-long patterns of being a victim. There is little respect for self. They are unable to say "no" and are not assertive. Because they cannot assert themselves, they are, in effect, abusing themselves by allowing themselves to be used and abused.

12. **Fear of Abandonment**

    - A survivor may become frantic when alone or when not in a relationship. There are unresolved feelings of dependency and a need to be taken care of.

13. **Fear of Gagging**

    - This fear can be related to being suffocated and controlled in the same way the perpetrator controlled the survivor.

14. Stress Reactions

- A crisis can cause an emotional shut-down and there may be a difficulty in coping with stressful situations.

15. Guilt

- Shame, self-blame, and a feeling of being responsible for the abuse is common among survivors. Because they feel guilty, they may have to take care of others to make up for being "bad." The need for punishment is manifested by getting into situations where victimization occurs.

16. Pseudo-maturity

- Child victims were not allowed to be children sexually and were thrust into adult sexuality before they were physically or emotionally ready. They can't seem to have fun and some say they have felt old all of their lives.

17. Difficulty in Feeling

- The survivor's feelings, needs, and wants are submerged because to feel is to experience pain and other difficult feelings. Because they are not in touch with who they are, they may feel like a non-person who is isolated from others. (I've seen cases where a survivor has no idea how to answer, "How are you feeling?" as they are not used to allowing themselves to be aware of their feelings.)

18. Need for Approval

- Survivors often have a desperate need to please other people, even at the expense of their own well-being. They are afraid that others will discover how "bad" they really are inside and try to keep themselves hidden by being subservient to others.

STATISTICS ARE SHOCKING

On the Forbes site, a report says that one out of every six women have been the victim of an attempted or complete rape in her lifetime, and about one in 33 of American men have experienced an attempted or complete rape in their lifetime.

Examples of beliefs of some people which work against a solution to widespread sexual misconduct in our culture (Southern Connecticut University site) include:

- Blaming the victim ("She asked for it")
- Trivializing sexual assault ("Boys will be boys")
- Sexually explicit jokes
- Tolerance of sexual harassment
- Inflating false rape report statistics
- Publicly scrutinizing a victim's dress, mental state, motive
- Dismissive if the victim is perceived as promiscuous or has "a past"
- Gratuitous gendered violence in movies and television
- Defining "manhood" as dominant and sexually aggressive
- Pressure on men to "score"
- Pressure on women to not appear "cold"
- Assuming that men do not get raped or that only "weak" men get raped
- Refusing to take rape accusations seriously
- Teaching people to avoid getting raped with emphasis that the victim has control over it happening or not

Victim-blaming attitudes marginalize the survivor and make it harder to come forward and report the abuse. If the survivor knows that you or society blames her/him for the abuse, she/he will not feel safe in coming forward and asking for help. Victim-blaming attitudes also reinforce what the abuser has been saying all along: that it is the victim's fault this is happening. It is NOT the victim's fault or responsibility to fix the situation. It is the abuser's chosen actions. By engaging in victim-blaming attitudes, society allows the abuser to perpetrate sexual assault while avoiding accountability of his/her actions. All of the people coming forward now is such a positive step to help reduce the incidents of sexual harassment and sexual assaults because it helps change attitudes from tolerance to intolerance—there is finally more agreement that abusers should be held accountable.

Again, we must learn and teach others that sexual assault is motivated by hostility, power, and control. Sexual assaults are not motivated by sexual desire. Many of those accused have accumulated power and feel they can use it to control and overpower others.

REPORTING SEXUAL HARASSMENT AND SEXUAL MISCONDUCT

Good information on how to proceed with sexual harassment issues can be found on The Find Law website. A summary of the process is:

Follow Your Employer's Policies and Procedures

1. If you are a victim of harassment, your first stop toward resolving the problem should be to let the offending party know you find their conduct offensive.

2. If the offensive conduct does not stop: Some companies have a process for handling sexual harassment claims. Keep a record of dates, times, persons involved, witnesses, and what was said.

3. If the company does not have a set procedure, put your report in writing to your supervisor. If the supervisor is the one who is harassing, go to his or her supervisor.

Administrative Charge

4. If you are unable to resolve your harassment complaint by using your employer's internal procedures, and if you wish to continue, you will need to file an administrative charge with the appropriate governmental agency, usually the Federal Equal Employment Opportunity Commission or your state's human rights or civil rights enforcement agency. The government agency will investigate your claim and will attempt to resolve it by negotiating with your employer.

5. If the agency cannot resolve your complaint, and it determines that your claim is a valid one, it will issue a "right of sue" letter. This letter means that you may bring your case to court.

Litigation

If the appropriate governmental agency issues a "right to sue" letter, you may bring a civil lawsuit for any injuries you suffered due to the sexual harassment. You do not need to show physical injuries. The most common injuries in a sexual harassment case are the emotional injuries suffered by the victim.

If your sexual harassment suit is successful, your remedies may include:

1. Re-instatement, if you lost your job

2. If you lost money or missed out on a raise, you are due three times that amount (for the time you have been out of work due to sexual harassment)

3. Fringe benefit lost

4. Damages for emotional stress

5. A requirement that your employer initiate policies or training to stop harassment

6. Pay for your attorney fees and court cost (Be sure to engage an experienced employee rights attorney in your area to discuss the facts of your particular situation and ensure that your legal rights are protected.)

What to Expect at a Criminal Trial

RAINN (Rape, Abuse, and Incest National Network) has a beautiful website that goes into great detail about what you can expect at a criminal trial. You may wish to read that networks very helpful information. I have summarized some of the information from their article "What to Expect at a Criminal Trial."

When a case against an alleged perpetrator goes to trial in criminal court, the victim often is asked to testify. A victim has rights:

- The right to apply for crime victim compensation
- The right to attend criminal justice proceedings
- The right to certain protections from intimidation and harassment throughout the trial
- The right to be heard and participate in criminal justice proceedings

You are entitled to:

Having a love one or friend with you during the proceedings

Support from a trained, local sexual assault service provider or the crime victim assistance organizations to be an advocate and support.

The site goes into who you will be talking to, your role as a witness, courtroom logistics, and tips for taking the stand. The end of a trial may bring a sense of relief or it may not offer the closure you were hoping for. You may need help from a therapist if you need more closure.

Again, there are many sites that offer you information about a court trial and it is advised that your attorney is the best resource of what is going to happen in court and what is expected of you.

FILING A CIVIL LAWSUIT – (Summary of AllLaw.com article)

Victims of sexual assault can, and often do, file a lawsuit against the perpetrator in civil court. Even though any kind of sexual assault incident can give rise to a criminal prosecution which can result in jail time, fines, probation, and other sanctions against the defendant if a conviction is obtained—a civil lawsuit is usually the only way that a sexual assault victim can get monetary compensation for harm suffered.

A jury may award very high damages. As a result, the perpetrator can be held liable to pay a lot of money. The unfortunate part is, if the defendant is not particularly wealthy, it may be very difficult, if not impossible, to collect. In some cases, a civil suit can be brought against another party in addition to the perpetrator of the assault. For example, if the incident occurred at a place of business, school or other institution, the entity (sometimes the perpetrator's employer) could also be liable based a negligent supervision claim or failure to provide adequate security. Ability to sue another party is probably an important factor in the huge settlements mentioned elsewhere in this chapter. Fox News and other companies generally have much larger resources than individuals.

Again, choose an attorney experienced in these type of cases and obtain your information from him or her.

ALLEGATIONS OF WOMEN
SEXUALLY HARASSING MEN AND BOYS

CHRISTINA GARCIA

From October, 2017, until February 8, 2018, the persons who were accused of sexual harassment and sexual assault were all men that were reported on any of the major websites.

Women commit acts of sexual harassment, assault, and abuse also.

On February 18, 2018, the Politico news site revealed that allegations had been made against Christina Garcia, a California assembly woman, by two male staff members.

She is accused of groping two male staff members (one of whom is now a prominent Sacramento lobbyist who does not want his name published) and making lewd sexual suggestions when apparently drunk. Both victims have reported and the investigation is underway by the California Assembly Rules Committee. Incidents were in 2012 and 2017, according to the Politico report.

She has been a high profile advocate of #MeToo and was featured in *Time Magazine* as one of the "Silence Breakers." Jessica Levison, professor of law at Loyola Law School of Los Angeles, says if the allegations are true, Christina is the "hypocrite of the century and that hypocrisy has no bounds." (Based on a report on Politico, 2/8/18.) Christina says she does not remember the incidents. Many women in the #Me, Too movement are concerned that her actions may cause damage to their cause.

Now that two men have bravely come forward with their allegations toward a high-profile woman, more men may file reports of their sexual harassment and sexual assault experiences with women. Harry Weinstein broke the ice regarding men assaulting women. The situation with Christina Garcia may break that same ice for men to report. Men in our culture have been raised to "take it like a man" and may consider themselves weak if they tell about being taken advantage of by being sexually harassed or sexually assaulted. I hope that men will now feel freer to help put an end to sexual assault the way that women have by speaking up.

While the vast majority of sexual harassment cases filed with the EEOC are filed by women, an increasing number of men are filing their own claims, according the PLBSH website. There are a number of cases involving female on male workplace sexual harassment that have resulted in significant awards for the male employees. These include instances of retaliations for refusing sexual advances, unwelcome touching and caressing and being subjected to offensive sexual comments and jokes. Male on male workplace sexual harassment claims are becoming more common, starting with a 1998 ruling from the United States Supreme Court that held that men also are protected from workplace sexual harassment.

Some men may not report their harassment or file a claim with the EEOC because they are afraid of being mocked by coworkers. They may believe that men cannot truly be sexually harassed by a woman, or that being harassed by another man implicates their own sexuality. They may be embarrassed if details of the harassment were leaked, particularly if they believe that they should be able to handle the issue themselves. Whatever the reason, it is evident that many men are not simply filing claims of sexual harassment.

HISTORY OF SEXUAL ASSAULT OF MALES BY WOMEN TEACHERS

There are a large number of women teachers who have been prosecuted for sexually assaulting males and females in their workplaces (schools) or outside of their schools. They, like men in companies, are using their power to entice under-age boys into sexual relationships.

The list of teachers is contained in a report "The 50 Most Infamous Female Teacher Sex Scandals" on the Zimbio website. Most have gone to prison and had very stiff consequences. Five examples of these cases:

Mary Kay Letourneau, age 34

> Sexual relationhip with a boy, age 13, who was in her sixth-grade class. Was prosecuted and went to prison for 7 years. She was married with children at the time. When she was released from prison in 2005, she married the boy and had two children with him. (1996)

Debra Lafave, age 23

> She was 23, the boy was 14. She was sentenced to 3 years house arrest and 7 years of probation for the sexual relationship with him. (2004)

Abbie Jane Swogg, age 34

> She had sexual relationships with several boys ages 14-17. Was sentenced to 7 years in jail and 36 years probation. (2009)

Pamela Rogers Turner, age 27

> She was sentenced to prison for 9 years for a sexual relationship with a 13-year-old boy. (2006)

Stephanie Rogers, age 28

> Sexual relationship with two boys, 14 and 16. Was given 10 years prison time and five years of probation. (Is smiling in her mug shots!) (2008)

Premature, coerced, or otherwise abusive or exploitive sexual experiences of the boys in the above cases were never positive with the teachers because the teachers were in a position of power over the boys. At a minimum, the boys likely felt confusion and insecurity. The experiences almost always harmed the boy's, and later on, the men's capacities for trust and intimacy and they were left with feelings of betrayal. However, boys and men often do not recognize the connections between what happened and their later emotional issues. To be used as a sexual object by a more powerful person, male or female, is never a good thing and can cause lasting harm.

CHAPTER 7

TREATMENT AND HEALING
FROM SEXUAL ABUSE

Children

Children who need treatment as a result of sexual abuse have symptoms of traumatic stress, depression and/or anxiety. It is common for children to blame themselves for the abuse or to feel that they could have prevented it. It is important to work with children around this belief and emphasize that they are not to blame for being abused. The child may be having difficulty in school or life because of the abuse.

If left untreated, if the abuse stops, the child's physical, mental and emotional health should improve to some degree, but the scars are deeper than you may realize if you have not personally experienced childhood sexual abuse. Invisible symptoms are often open wounds that lead to dysfunctional teen and adult relationships, addictive behaviors with drugs, sex, alcohol, or other ways of numbing the pain. On the other hand, if the child is removed from the abuse and also treated as soon as possible, the outlook for healing and leading a healthy, happy life is more optimistic.

Below is an example of one kind of therapy for children who have been sexually abused. There are other agencies and kinds of therapy that you can also consider; the important thing is to get professional help for any abused child, as soon as possible.

The National Center for Child Traumatic Stress (NCCN) in Pennsylvania believes that a treatment called "Trauma–Focused Cognitive-Behavioral Therapy" is empirically validated treatment for child sexual abuse that has evolved as the clear standard of care for children and adolescents who have experienced abuse and trauma. NCCN can refer you to a practitioner who is highly experienced in treating child trauma including victims of sexual abuse. Judith Cohen, MD, a member of NCCN, writes:

1. The child and caregiver are educated in common reactions and symptoms that may result from sexual abuse. This helps children understand that their reactions and feelings are normal and that treatment can help them. It helps non-abusing parents to accept that the abuse was not their fault nor the child's fault.

2. Another step is to help the child to identify his or her negative feelings such as anxiety, jumpiness, and sadness that can occur after a trauma. The therapist gives the child techniques to modulate these feelings and to soothe him or herself. This is important so that the child does not begin to withdraw from life to avoid having these feelings.

3. Another part of the treatment helps children to analyze the connections between their thoughts and feelings and behavior. Children who have been sexually abused often feel bad about themselves. They may blame themselves or believe that nothing good will ever happen to them again. They are encouraged to explore their thoughts, beliefs, and feelings about the abuse.

4. Another part is overcoming learned fears. This means unlearning the connection a child has made between the abuse, his or her negative feelings about it and trauma reminders, other things and events that he or she has associated with the experience. Desensitization may be necessary when a child continues to have intense reactions to particular things, places, people or situations that remind him or her of the trauma. For instance, if he or she was sexually abused in a basement, they may be encouraged to imagine a basement without feeling upset. Then the therapist may even accompany the child to a basement.

5. The child tells the story of the abuse, i.e., how it happened, how it felt and what it meant. By putting his or her memories in order, the child no longer feels haunted by them.The therapist helps identify and correct the child's distorted ideas and beliefs about the abuse. For example, an adolescent was in treatment for abuse that had occurred when she was five years old and the perpetrator was 15. She was still blaming herself for "letting" the abuse

occur. By creating the trauma narrative, she realized she had been blaming herself for something she had not had the power to prevent. By telling the story to her therapist, she corrected her own false understanding.

A child who has been sexually abused needs to be evaluated for possible therapy. Getting a child help is so important if they need it so that they do not have to carry around issues caused by the abuse and be affected by them for years. It is important to do careful research including recommendations from other professionals such as doctors, educators, etc. when investigating child therapy resources.

Adults

Survivors of sexual abuse that happened either when they were children or as adults may believe that it is better not to rehash the past. They may avoid feelings and memories in order to focus on tasks at hand and function in their day-to-day lives. However, the abuse may still be affecting them and preventing them from living a happy and full life. Often, the survivor fears for his or her life or physical well-being and feels that there is no choice but to do what the attacker wants. But submission does not equal consent. If a survivor submits, it does not mean that he or she agreed to, or accepted the situation. A survivor is never responsible for being sexually abused. The responsibility for the abuse lies with the perpetrator. Sexual abuse is committed primarily by a perpetrator who needs to feel powerful and in control by forcing or coercing someone else to participate in unwanted sexual activity.

As the saying goes, the truth will set you free. Some adults go to a therapist for relationship and other issues and do not even hint at past abuse for a long time. They may doubt their own memories or feel too fragile to come out of denial. If you have been sexually abused, it is very important to believe you were sexually abused as a child or/and as an adult…and that it was not your fault. Then you can make a decision to heal. When you recognize the effects of sexual abuse in your life, you need to make a strong commitment to heal and to have a willingness to change. You will be dealing with memories and suppressed feelings which can be disorienting; however, you will realize during therapy that eventually these feelings can and will be resolved.

Many survivors suppress some memories of what has happened to them in childhood as well as with a traumatic event in their adult life such as date rape, stranger rape, marital rape, incest, sexual abuse from those outside of your family, sodomy, voyeurism, indecent exposure, pornography, or sexual harassment. Those who forget parts of incidents also forget the feeling associated with them. Remembering is the process of getting back both the memory and feelings. Some survivors often doubt their own perceptions. Starting to believe that the incidents were really sexually abusive and damaging and that it really hurt is an important part of the healing process. Some survivors of sexual abuse as children and/or adults have kept the abuse a secret. Telling another about what happened is a powerful healing force that can alleviate the shame of being a victim. Getting in touch with their vulnerability can help the survivor feel compassion for self, more anger at the abuser, and greater closeness with others. They need to learn to trust their own own perceptions and feelings and have more trust in themselves. As children and adults struggling to survive, many survivors have not felt their pain which can heal. Grieving is a way to acknowledge pain, let go, and move into the present. Anger is a powerful force which the survivor can direct at the abuser and those who did not protect him or her. The anger is an emotion that is very helping in healing. As the survivor moves through their healing, they will reach a point of resolution. While history cannot be erased, the survivor will be making important changes in his or her life. There will be more of an awareness of life and compassion toward themselves and others.

I am most certain that survivors cannot heal from sexual assault unless they are willing to face the truth, talk about it, share their stories with empathic others, grieve their loss of trust and sense of security in the world and feel their pain and until he or she has completed the process of grief. In order to face the truth, defense mechanisms must be realized. These have the faces of denial that the abuse was harmful, minimization that it was as damaging as it was, forgiving too soon as a way of avoiding the pain feeling, drinking, drugging, sexual or other addictions to avoid the pain, intellectualizing to know what happened but not feel the pain and a variety of other creative methods of numbing reality.

Sexual abuse may influence the survivor's ability to establish and maintain a healthy sexual relationship. It may take time to develop a positive sexual concept and it is important to begin the journey slowly and trust themselves. Sexual healing may not be as fast as survivors and intimate partners would wish. Sexual healing is a profound personal growth work. Addressing sexual issues is often seen as the final stage in sexual abuse recovery. You may wish to work with a therapist or coach who specializes in sexual abuse treatment.

Survivors can greatly benefit from joining a therapy or support group. Recovery is possible and very probable. Healing may take weeks, months, and even years. Everyone's healing journey is different. Despite the ample media and political assault revelations these days, there has not been a whole lot of discourse about the surviving part of being a survivor...the part where the survivor pieces his or her life back together and starts regaining the happiness and control that the abuser tried to take away from them.

Sexual assault can change your feelings about yourself and those around you. You may not feel the way you did before the assault. Individual counseling and group counseling can help deal with those issue and aid in recovery.

Support Groups

Being with other survivors is very important in your healing process and joining a group with other women and men is a great way for you to work through issues with others who have been abused. There is support there as well and input from others on problem solving. Other survivors are able to help you deal with whatever your issues are. Many group members find inspiration and motivation in the stories of other survivors.

The group is able to get together on a regular schedule to support each other in healing. I believe it is very important to have a trained-in-sexual-abuse-issues therapist or coach facilitate the group. In a group you are able to share your feelings, your struggles and your strength. You are able to appreciate the beautiful qualities of others in the group. Sometimes we are blaming ourselves for our abuse and through being with others you can clearly see that it is not their fault that they were abused and that they are not to blame. You can be compassionate about their struggles and have a kindness toward them that you have not extended yet to yourself. As you realize you are like others in your group, you learn to view yourself in a more positive way. You are able to reach out and make friends that are there to support you perhaps even after you are no longer part of the group.

Male Survivor Lack of Support Groups

Though more girls and women are victims of sexual abuse than boys and men, there have been historically few recovery options for male survivors. Even in major metropolitan areas, support groups dedicated to male survivors—which are a key way for survivors to find healing—are challenging to find. While there may be dozen of support groups for female survivors within any given city, there are often les than five for men. The numbers become even more bleak as you move into less populated areas.

Group support is not the only area lacking resources. Male survivors have long struggled to find therapists and other clinicians who are trained and knowledgeable in the specific issues facing men who have been abused. A therapist who is uninformed about male survivor issues may not know, for instance, that victims may experience erections or even ejaculation during abuse or rape, as a matter of reflex. Survivors need to be assured that an erection or ejaculation is not the same as giving consent for sexual abuse, and a therapist who questions whether an experience was consensual may exacerbate a survivor's same, pushing him further into silence and suffering.

For so many survivors, disclosing an abuse story is challenging enough—and taking the risk with a therapist who isn't familiar with the issues can make the experience more traumatic than therapeutic. I was reading about a man who was trying to find a support group for male survivors, he was referred to a support group for sex offenders, suggesting that he might find some help there. It is difficult to imagine how anybody could think that a survivor of sexual abuse should be trying to heal alongside convicted sex criminals.

Considering how many men are survivors, and the damaging mental and physical health effects it has on its victims, what are the reasons why there is so much secrecy surround male sexual abuse—especially compared to our relative openness in discussing abuse of women and girls? Traditional masculine identity is often dependent upon "toughness." We educate our boys from the time they're young that they need to man up. We expect that they push down their feelings in favor of appearing strong and impervious to emotions, and we punish boys for sensitivity and tears. This culture of invincibility is far from welcoming to a boy or man who needs to talk about having been harmed and being a victim.

With all of the sexual harassment reports that women have made in the media recently, I have not read one report from a male who was sexually harassed by a woman or man. Sexual harassment is not just a woman's issue alone, although it seems to happen less frequently to a male. I wonder how many men have been sexually harassed and not reported it because they do not want to be thought of as a victim and, therefore, not masculine and weak, unable to defend himself. Male survivors need as much compassion as women survivors, however males in our culture are getting less. The media may be slowly turning the abuse of boys and men into a conversation that people are willing to have, releasing some of the taboo

There are online resources available to male survivors which are a godsend to them. One excellent online resource is www.1in6.com The name of the website explains that 1 in 6 males are sexually abused as children. Online support can be life-saving for male survivors, but the end goal for the organizations doing this work is that men will be able to walk into rooms where they are accepted, and find community and support in person. If this can happen, and many believe that it can, many more men and boys can hopefully come to terms with their abuse at younger ages.

Individual Counseling

It is important that the survivor find a counselor or coach with whom he or she feel respected, valued, and understood. The counselor can help them with their fear of being vulnerable, feelings of anger, betrayal, being violated, shame, guilt, embarrassment, powerlessness, feeling violated, and symptoms of Post Stress Trauma Disorder. PSTD is an anxiety disorder that developes, after a person is exposed to a terrifying event or ordeal in which grave physical harm occurred or was threatened. Survivors of rape often suffer RTS meaning Rape Trauma Syndrome which is a fear of death while being raped. The survivor needs to understand that rape can happen to anyone no matter who they are and that the rape was not their fault in any way. They need to know that they cannot accept blame for being an innocent victim. The counselor does not minimize their experiences and there is a warmth between the survivor and counselor. It is important that the counselor is very well versed in sexual abuse issues and fully respects feelings such as grief, anger, sadness, joy, and any other feeling that comes up. When the survivor trusts a counselor to support his or her healing, they are allowing the counselor to know them and profoundly touch his or her life. He or she should be honored to be a part of the healing process and give the best of his or her skills, experience and compassion. The survivor and counselor area team which enables healing, growing and going forth into a happy and fulfilled life.

You learn that you have nothing to be ashamed of and that you are in no way to blame for being abused that that you have every right to reclaim your life, to move on and experience the world in all of its radiant splendor. Once we feel and heal our pain, we are fully able to experience the awesome joy of life.

WRITING TO HEAL (JOURNALING)

As a part of your healing from sexual abuse, you may wish to keep a journal to help you clarify your thoughts and feelings and gain perspective on your sexual abuse experiences. It can be a way to process the traumatic elements of your abuse in a safe way. Try taking some time to write about what happened and how you are feeling about everything. Do not worry about it making sense or being grammatically correct—this journal is just for you. Most survivors have something they wish they could say to someone they can't—for instance confronting their abuser or telling a loved one about the abuse, A journal can be a safe way to do that. Try writing a letter to that person in your journal, saying everything you wish you could tell them You do not need to send the letter or even show it to anyone, and sometimes destroying it by ripping it up into small pieces or safely burning it can feel cathartic. The following two writings from Bobbi and Maggie helped them feel their power and propel them toward healing.

BOBBI'S STORY

I have permission to share with you an award-winning essay by "Bobbi." Writing has helped her immensely, and she wants people to know it can be not only therapeutic but an enjoyable creative exercise as well. She tells me that her experience of abuse as a child did more to shape her personality, character, relationships, ability to parent, and self view than anything else in her six decades of life. Hers has been a life of struggling to accept, heal, and move beyond the scars of her childhood. Certainly one reason she had so many problems is that she never told anyone of the abuse until thirty years after the experience. Then, motivated by her love and protectiveness of her own young daughters, she went to a therapist. For the first time, Bobbi told her parents about her grandfather sexually abusing her from 5-10 years of age. The abuse took place in his woodworking shop. For her, and for many adults, there is no "completely getting over it." At least not yet. This book is for Bobbi, and others, but also for every one of us that can help *prevent* abuse, thus eliminating the need for deep psychological help and years and years of healing.

*   *   *

Sawdust

Papa took me out to his workshop every evening after our early dinner. My grandmother never came with us. Maybe her knees were so bad with arthritis, the five-minute walk was too much for her. Or maybe she didn't want to face her suspicion of what was going on out there.

Papa's shop was a grey cement-block building which stood alone near the sidewalk's end, past the water tanks. Inside the shop: gray walls, brown wood, black tool handles. The smell of varnish hung in the hot sticky air. A black rubber mat on the gray cement floor was the only décor. A centered, plywood table supported a lathe, its cold metal machine voice steely silent. Sometimes the table top was covered with wood pieces and their wide-jawed clamps, two-clawed hammers, jagged-tooth saws. Sometimes a freshly varnished captain's chair perched on the table like it had jumped up there off the floor.

One hot, humid, July day, Papa was working on one of his famous tea carts. My big brother and I were together in Papa's shop, a rare event. My brother picked up a power tool off the worktable and examined it, turning it slowly in his hands. A stop sign flashed in my mind as if I had reached for the tool myself. I of course wasn't allowed to touch a power tool. "You got no business with that, little girl," I heard a scolding replay in my mind. I reached out and snatched the yardstick which was leaning against the workbench and clenched my hand as tight as my teeth.

"....my new jigsaw," Papa explained to my brother. I held the yardstick, the worn wooden flat stick almost too big around for my grip. Tap, tap, tap. I tapped the edge on the cement floor next to the faded cane back chair. Scrape, scrape, scrape. I dragged the stick through the shavings and sawdust and pushed up spoonfuls of it to make a tidy hill.

I knew the shavings by heart. Each was a variation of blondish brown, each with a hundred edges. I knew the edges of the shavings, some sliced smooth, some rough torn. I knew the dust that covered the edges of the shavings; some fine and powder light, some coarse and as big as a splinter. Studying the sawdust was what I did, standing by the old cane back chair for endless amounts of time, yesterday, the day before that, as long as I can remember. Only the creaking cane back chair that my grandfather sat in broke my keen concentration on the sawdusty floor. My eyes, my mind, my soul, had been on that floor many, many times, so I knew it well.

In a slightly delayed reaction, I heard my brother's words, and was startled to realize they were directed at me. "Aunt Martha was lovin' her tea cart when we were there, Sunday, wasn't she?" I looked up into his handsome face, noticing like always his beautiful smooth skin, not your typical teenager skin, no blemishes, clean-shaven. His soft blue eyes connected with mine and held my look. I nodded the expected response and said "Uh-huh." He unlocked our eyes and went back to his friendly conversation with the diseased man he was immune to.

My gaze drifted and stopped on Papa's straw hat hanging on the wall. I put one bended knee on the chair's seat and pressed it down hard to lift myself to reach the edge of the hat. With the hat in my hand, I walked away from the chair and sat down on the floor. While Papa worked and chatted with my brother, I scraped the edge of my small cupped hand along the cold, rough floor. I closed it around one tiny mound and then the next, and filled the bottom of the upside down hat with saw dust, wood chips, and dusty shavings off the floor.

"Papa," I interrupted my brother. I held the hat out to Papa. "Put on your hat, Papa," I said. With no hesitation, he took the hat from my hands and turned it over while putting it on top of his sweaty head. The insides dumped out. Fine dust, coarse shavings, and dirty scrapings rained down over his sweaty brow and nose. A cloud of sawdust covered his entire face and the tiny chips stuck there, or fell to his shoulders. He squinted and blinked his eyes, his eyelashes now covered in coarse yellow dust.

My brother yelled at me, "I've never seen anyone do anything so MEAN!" His face was red and his voice shook with anger.

I looked at the shavings and dust covering Papa's tightly closed eyes. He sputtered to blow the sticky shavings off his lips and mouth. He reached up with one large, mottled-skin hand and removed the hat from his head. More dust rained from his mouse-grey hair onto his shoulders, which had started to slump forward.

Shame burned my eyes and made them water. I hated what had just happened, but I hated Papa more. I stared at Papa. He looked pathetic. Instead of feeling sorry, I started feeling a rush. I felt triumphant, and finally, in control.

Papa never said a word.

*   *   *

MAGGIE'S LETTER

When I was 8 and my brother was 16 and babysitting me, he coaxed me into performing oral sex on him. This was something so traumatic that I suppressed it until I was 23, when the memory of the incident came flooding back. Reading books on the subject and talking to fellow survivors were the first two things that made it clear that I had many symptoms of being an incest survivor.

I do not at all believe that to heal, one must confront their abuser. But in my case I decided to do that. I wrote my brother an 8-page letter and mailed it off. As it turned out, I was one of the lucky ones, because it did feel like his reply was very healing to me. He acknowledged the incident, took full responsibility for it, apologized, and said he would do anything I wanted to help heal from it. It definitely felt like a weight lifted off my shoulders. Journaling about my feelings was also a key part of dealing with them. And finally, I found psychotherapy to be a lifesaver.

My psychotherapist was well-trained in bringing about healing from sexual abuse, and knew how to dig deeper into how it had affected my sense of self-worth and also my relationships. Healing from this incident, and other sexual abuse incidents in my childhood as well, was not something I felt I could have done alone. Incest can have a way of making you feel very alone in the first place, and estranged from your own family. To have a supportive, compassionate therapist in a confidential setting to safely discuss all the details, and especially to validate my feelings, was invaluable–especially because the healing is not always linear, and you never know how and when the issues are going to resurface. In the end, I feel that I have put most of the hurt behind me.

It has been proven that writing and/or journaling assists survivors to heal and progress on their path to thriving. You can find workshops, ask your therapist for suggested guides or books, or look at any major bookseller to find excellent resources for yourself or someone you know. Here are a few examples:

The Courage to Heal: A Guide for Women Survivors of Child Sexual Abuse, 20th Anniversary,

by Ellen Bass and Laura Davis

Writing to Heal: A guided journal for recovering from trauma & emotional upheaval,

by James W. Pennebaker

Opening Up by Writing It Down, Third Edition: How Expressive Writing Improves Health and Eases Emotional Pain, by James W. Pennebaker

OTHER STORIES OF HOPE AND HEALING
FROM SURVIVORS

I found some wonderful stories of hope and healing written by sexual abuse/assault survivors on the web site of RAINN (Rape, Abuse and Incest National Network) and felt you would be inspired! I have summarized their stories, however have fully related to you their messages of hope and healing in their own words.

The survivors that are written about are part of RAINN's speakers bureau. I have quoted their messages for you.

Scott's Story

When Scott was 11, his mother's boyfriend began abusing he and his sister. The abuse went on for two years and became very frequent. When he told his dad about the sexual abuse, the dad immediately reported the abuse to the police. The perpetrator went to prison. He found out that his mother knew about the abuse but did not step in to stop it. He had to go to court to testify against the boyfriend which was painful.

Scott said, "I go to church regularly. Connecting with my faith was important for me learning how to heal." He hopes to open his own Christian-based non-profit one day to help men with similar experiences. Today, Scott is thriving. He has a successful business as a TV director and controller and a family with children he adores. When times are tough, he takes to the outdoors to help him relax. He shares his story proudly, but it wasn't always easy to talk about what happened. "I joined RAINN's Speaker's Bureau to help me get my story out there. When I was a child and everything happened, I thought I was the only one. I want men to know there is help out there, and plenty of guys who have been through the same thing."

Stephanie's Story

Stephanie was sexually abused by her uncle on a regular basis between the ages of 4 and 12. Her parents both worked full-time and she was left in the care of her uncle and grandmother. Her grandmother caught the abuse happening once early on but did not tell Stephanie's parents because she was afraid they would not let her babysit anymore. The uncle threatened her so she would not tell anyone. She also had to testify against her uncle in court when she reported the abuse to the police several years later. She felt traumatized about testifying. She went into counseling and began speaking to groups about sexual abuse while in college.

Stephanie views the abuse as an obstacle she overcame, not as something that defines her as a person. She is married with a family and is a senior manager at her company and is surrounded by a supportive community. She said, "What I tell people when I give speeches is that if you are dealing with something like this, find someone to talk to. If you don't find a good outlet at first, keep trying. It is not a burden you should carry and you should not have to suffer alone. There is a lot of life to live and it gets better"

Danyol's Story

Danyol was sexually abused and raped repeatedly by his older cousin between the ages of 7-10. He told his family who did either not believe it or did not want him to talk about it. He had a lot of pain and issues when he joined a group therapy group in high school that his counselor suggested.

His healing process has been helped with the support of his best friend for the last 15 years, connection to his faith, and artistic expression. Danyol created a one-man dramatic stage play about abuse and self discovery. He wanted to tell his story in his own way to reclaim the power of sharing what happened with him to his family and friends. Danyol advocates for ways in which family friends can be more supportive when a survivor discloses abuse. He recommends not pressuring the survivors into giving detailed information about their abuse. This forces them into reliving the incident and can cause repeated trauma. Danyol instead suggests letting them share aspects of their story when they are ready and showing your support through believing their story. He is pursuing a career in the entertainment industry and finishing his autobiography. It has been important to Danyol to use his voice to empower other survivors to tell their stories when they are ready. He said, "Talking about it really does take back power from the trauma."

Sharon's Story

Sharon was assaulted, abused and repeatedly raped by her husband over the course of four years. It started out with controlling behavior and emotional abuse and escalated to increasingly violent physical and sexual assault. "There was a lot of self-blame for staying in the situation. A lot of self doubt. I worried about the perception others would have of me." After many horrific experiences, she reported the abuse to the police. He fled the country.

She has found counseling helpful along with an emotional support animal to be useful during her healing process. "The biggest thing for me was when I got to the point where I could let go of responsibility for my husband's actions. I held myself accountable for a long time." She is raising her son and focuses on teaching him about respect, good touch/bad touch and correct terms for body parts. She wants him to grow up knowing he is in control of his body. She continues to work in victim advocacy and is considering going back to school for her master's degree. She says "For someone in a similar situation, there is help out there. Don't lose hope"

Alison's Story

Alison woke up to find a perpetrator in her home. The hours that followed were traumatic; he raped her at gunpoint multiple times, robbed her of her possessions, and forced her to withdraw money at an ATM. She felt paralyzed and disassociated from reality. She went to the home of her parents after she escaped and contacted the police immediately. "The detective who worked on my case was trained specifically for sex crimes, which made a big difference," said Alison. For the next year, Alison worked with law enforcement officials to help convict the perpetrator. The process was very hard. "I could have done better with self care when it was all happening," she says. "But I did get free counseling through a local sexual assault service provider and that helped" Working within the criminal justice system was difficult but she did it.

Today Alison spends her free time dancing and practicing yoga to stay on top of self-care. She also shares her story with the media and other survivors in the hopes of lifting the veil off the criminal justice process. "It is never going away. So I am not going to stop. I am going to keep doing this kind of work with RAINN and hope that it makes a difference."

Kassie's Story

Kassie was sexually assaulted by a stranger at the Florida State University library while at her work-study job. She was attacked when a young man, not an FSU student, attacked her from behind. He was armed, choked her and raped her. She reported the incident immediately and the FSU police came to the library immediately but did not provide Kassie with the support she needed. "Something like this had never happened on campus. Not like my situation. They were not sure how to handle it." The case went to trial one year after she was assaulted and he is serving a life sentence in prison. In a Victim Impact Statement she read at the trial, Kassie forgave her attacker. "Some would feel hopelessness. But not me. I feel so sorry for you. Because instead of choosing to be a productive member of society you chose to rape and murder innocent people... I am sorry the life path you chose has led you down this dark alley."

At first Kassie found it scary to share her story, but later noticed that it helped her heal from the trauma. "After you share and get good feedback, you start wanting to share more. Counseling has also been a helpful resource. When it first happened to me, I got into counseling. You should tell somebody. It doesn't matter who—go to a friend, mom, dad, or teacher. If you can't report to the police, tell someone you trust. That really helped me." She continued, "Everybody who interacts with students and the representatives of the university definitely should be trained in victimology." She also points out that is also important to talk with students about sexual violence. She now works at the Smithsonian Museum and volunteers at a rape crisis center and finds it fulfilling to help others as she has been helped.

WISDOM OF HEALING

Many survivors and thrivers of trauma actually realize that they have learned some valuable wisdom. They have found their inner strength and resolve, tenacity and hope. Without embracing denial, reality can be faced, challenged, grived, and accepted. The survivor of sexual abuse picks themselves up and discovers that he or she is whole. She or he goes forward with self-empowerment and is able to face the rest of his or her life with determination.

A survivor learns to self-nurture by providing themselves with good food, getting regular exercise, sleeping enough, connecting with others, nurturing relationships with people who make them feel good about themselves, and making it a priority to spend time with friends and family. Relaxation techniques or meditation are important to help manage life stress. It is important to find time to do activities they enjoy and get involved in a sport or hobby. It is good to join a group of those who share interests and connect with others. We all need people. Social contact can make a survivor feel less isolated and more connected. Supportive listeners can include friends, family, religious leaders, teachers, as well as counselors in individual counseling and counseling groups.

Healing is a work in progress with the survivor turning the tide and beginning a new life. The survivor realizes that while they have a vulnerability to be hurt, she or he becomes more kind, compassionate, empathic, and understanding to others as well as to him- or herself.

Survivors come to realize that they:

Have come from victim to victory

Refer to themselves as "overcomers"

Have gotten in touch with their irrepressible spirits

Have moved from "survivors" to "survivors victorious"

My message to survivors and thrivers is beautifully expressed by the poet, Rumi.

"The wound is the place where light enters you."

—Rumi

ACKNOWLEDGMENTS

John Salveson—I so appreciate the incredible and insightful foreword you wrote for this book. I admire you so much.

My four sons and their families—I am so blessed by having a beautiful family. Family is everything.

My clients—Love and appreciation to all of the courageous and powerful individuals who have given me so much.

John Baxter—Thank you for editing my research and writings on the topic of sexual abuse many years ago and supporting me in my mission to educate as many people as possible on this topic.

Women's Resource Center in Wayne, Pennsylvania—Deep gratitude for all of the wonderful clients you referred to me and the support you offered me in making a difference in people's lives. I am still in touch with some of them.

All of my beautiful friends—What would I do without any of you? You all indeed are "the wind beneath my wings."

Barbara Dee—My editor and publisher, thank you for partnering with me to make my dream of a book on sexual abuse become a reality. I appreciate all of your skills going through the process. Know that you are part of the significant difference I hope this book makes in the world.

ABOUT THE AUTHOR

Susan Sophie Bierker, MSW and Sexual Abuse Prevention Advocate, has an extensive background as a Licensed Clinical Social Worker in Pennsylvania, in private practice for 20 years. She is an expert in the field of sexual abuse. Prior to the counseling practice, she was a social worker for Children and Youth Services in Media, Pennsylvania, where she counseled youth and their families, including children and teenagers who had been emotionally, physically and/or sexually abused. Her private practice provided individual, couple, and group therapy. In addition to extensive training and experience in the treatment of child victims and adult survivors of sexual abuse. Bierker's expertise includes counseling men and women who are experiencing any traumatic life events.

In practice as a Life Coach since moving to Florida, she helps sexual abuse victims and those experiencing trauma become not only survivors but also thrivers who go on to live fuller, happier lives. One of her missions in life is to help those who are hurting and confused to heal and move on with their lives, and do it joyfully. Her other mission and life's purpose is to provide education about sexual abuse to as many people as she can, because education is the most important step on the journey toward prevention. She encourages everyone to get educated, pay attention, and help others, so they too can be a Sexual Abuse Prevention Advocate.

In addition to providing sexual abuse education to various organizations, including police departments, school systems,, hospitals and other community groups. Bierker has appeared on radio talk shows to discuss sexual abuse. She has several published writings on sexual abuse.

To contact Susan Sophie Bierker, please visit

www.metoosexualabuse.com

CPSIA information can be obtained
at www.ICGtesting.com
Printed in the USA
LVOW13s1419240718
584763LV00018B/494/P